Essay Index

FORCES IN FICTION
AND OTHER ESSAYS

FORCES IN FICTION AND OTHER ESSAYS

BY RICHARD BURTON

Essay Index Reprint Series

 BOOKS FOR LIBRARIES PRESS
FREEPORT, NEW YORK

First Published 1902
Reprinted 1969

STANDARD BOOK NUMBER:
8369-0008-1

LIBRARY OF CONGRESS CATALOG CARD NUMBER:
70-76896

FOR PERMISSION TO REPRINT THE PAPERS IN THIS VOLUME THANKS ARE DUE TO THE EDITORS OF THE FORUM, THE BOOKBUYER, THE PHILADELPHIA SATURDAY EVENING POST, THE INDEPENDENT, THE CRITERION, AND THE NEW ENGLAND MAGAZINE.

CONTENTS

FORCES IN FICTION

AND

OTHER ESSAYS

THE FUNDAMENTALS OF FICTION

Good novel-making, technically viewed, rests
four-square upon invention (plot), construction,
characterization, and description. These may be
called the fundamentals of fiction. The form of
literature known as the story is often spoken of
carelessly or in shallow wise as if its manner—its
style or diction—were the chief thing, even the
only thing. "Have you read so and so?" queries
one lady of another in the car. "The idea isn't
anything, but then, you know, Brown writes so
well! His style is so good!" Again, with the
great class of uncritical readers, represented in the
lower grade by the blue-clothed messenger boy in
the car immersed in the latest number of the
"Fireside Companion," plot outweighs every other
consideration. Possibly it does with the majority
of all novel-lovers.

But if, looking to the permanent successes and
great names of fiction, we ask ourselves what
qualities constitute the essentials of fiction, we

shall be likely to settle on these fundamental four. Furthermore, if forced to pick out the quality ministering most to the successful result, we must, I fancy, reply: character-creation. This judgment may fall strange on the ear nowadays, because other traits are emphasized—construction or style, for example. Indeed, if we examine the clever work of present-day novelists, we shall find that what often gives them reputation is ability in ways aside from this central, this solar, gift of characterization. Compared with it, invention and construction are secondary; description and style, important as they may be in the abstract, are as naught. A novel without salient character-drawing, whatever its merits in other directions, can never take high rank; it is almost certainly a failure foredoomed.

The truth of the proposition becomes apparent when we come to apply it and illustrate by it. The firm, steady hold upon the public of certain fictionists, who are more or less roughly handled by critics, is easily explained, if we agree to this central place of importance held by character-limning. Master improvisers like Dumas and Scott showed their genius just here. Their personages live; the robust types they created are realized to the imaginations of readers; so that to kill off the sense of their existence would literally leave the actual world lonelier for many of us. The folk next door are real; we know it in a perfunctory way. But they are phantoms compared with the verity of the Three Guardsmen, or of Di Vernon and Dandie Dinmont.

Dickens, to take a later novelist, is perhaps the best possible example of this paramount power which excuses shortcomings in other directions. Is there any other maker of story in modern English literature—after all allowances have been made, and not forgetting that some current criticism of the man of Gadshill will have it that he is for a more careless age—who has begun to furnish such a portrait-gallery of worthies and adorable grotesques—a motley crowd whom we all know and enjoy and love? I wot not. The fact that Dickens is at times a trifle inchoate or careless in his English, or allows his exuberance to lead him into exaggeration, or fails to blend perfectly the discordant elements of comedy and tragedy, sinks into insignificance when set over against such a faculty as this. He was a veritable giant here.

Scott, too, was by no means firm-handed in the matter of construction; his huddled endings so-called—that is, his inability to close a book in due proportion to its main action and in a way to make the issue seem inevitable—must be conceded to critical scrutiny. The reason of it lies in this same power he had in character-conception. When he had fully sketched in his types, had presented them full-view to the audience, his interest in their case waned a little. Hence he was not so adept in getting rid of them neatly, as the novelist with an eye to a good finish must be, unless he supinely adopt the invertebrate method of a Henry James and dismiss the notion of any plot or argument at all for the story, which may be high art, but is chilling in effect upon the patrons. The very methods of work of the Abbotsford Sage were inimical to the highest results of construction. He did not make a *scenario,* blocking out his work and seeing it in the round as he began to write. Rather, his imagination fired by a scene or a character, he reeled off page after page of manuscript, throwing them upon the floor, with no thought of revision.

Dickens, for his part, was all his days under the bondage of serial publication. He wrote with twenty-parts in mind; and his tales would have been different in length, management, and even in the number of actors, had he been independent of this practical restriction. One has only to read "Forster's Life" to be impressed by this fact. It was not until comparatively late in his career that he gave much care to the matter of construction. To see how an artistic conscience developed in him with experience, compare early works such as "Pickwick Papers" and "Nicholas Nickleby" with a late success, "Great Expectations."

Fecundity of invention may or may not consist with this most precious gift of character-creation. Scott no doubt may be said to have had a decided instinct for fable, even for plot. Dickens possessed it in a less degree. Books containing his masterpieces of humorous portraiture—"Chuzzle-wit," "Dombey," "Bleak House," and "Copper-field" are in illustration—are either slight or loose-jointed or unconvincing as to plot. The story in which above all others he tried avowedly to substitute serious incident for wealth of char-acterization, "The Tale of Two Cities," has never ranked among his major performances. "Great Expectations" is almost his only book of which it may be declared that a well-conceived fable is suc-cessfully handled. Yet Dickens certainly had a feeling for plot. It would be more accurate, therefore, to say that he never quite gained as-sured mastery in the proper manipulation of the story-strands. "Little Dorrit," for example, is a comparative failure, not so much because its seri-ous idea—the fortunes of the Dorrits in relation to the mystery of Mrs. Clennam—fails in inter-est, as because the ample satiric characterization, centering around the Circumlocution Office, over-loads and confuses the story. This great writer was too rich in comic inspiration not to be led into digressions and all sorts of fascinating departures, complicating the movement of the narrative, but, at the same time, and to the everlasting advantage of the world of readers, widening the field of ob-servation and enriching fiction with relishable pictures of humanity.

With Thackeray, plot is always secondary and, for the most part, noticeably slight. So true is this that, assuming incident to be a requisite of the novel, "Vanity Fair" and "Pendennis" are hardly to be called novels at all; being, rather, satiric social sketches. In "Esmond," which as an historical romance demands plot more than his other studies of life, the same lack is easily recognized. It is characterization first, last, and all the time, with Thackeray. Thousands know Becky Sharp intimately who would be hard put to it to outline the plot in which she is a protagonist. The naturalness, distinctness, and variety of his character-types are the qualities which claim our regard and admiration; and vastly dissimilar as Dickens is from his great fellow of the earlier Victorian fiction, much the same description applies to him.

In point of style, it is the fashion to laud Thackeray at the expense of the other; and that, artist against artist, the preference is right enough cannot be denied. Dickens was always an unequal writer of English; and there is no book of his which as a whole does not reveal carelessnesses, of which Thackeray was seldom, if ever, guilty. But, I would venture to say, the contrast has been exaggerated. He of Gadshill commanded a diction of extraordinary vigor and idiomatic freshness and vivacity. Why should we not see it and say it? With a natural gift for expression, his reading in his youth was wonderfully well adapted to future results. He saturated himself with Richardson, Fielding, and Smollett, with Addison and Steele. It gave him a grip on the vernacular, which grew stronger with the years. He wrote all through his career under the goad, and had the demerits of the hasty producer; but to speak as if Dickens had no grace or force of diction— and the position has been fashionable of late—is simply nonsense. He often surpasses the writer who is more correct, just in proportion as the idiomatic is more precious than the merely proper.

The only other major novelist of the Victorian mid-century, George Eliot, furnishes further food for reflection. The clear-eyed and sure-handed way in which she presents the middle-class country types, this it is which gives her so unassailable a place. When one thinks of her stories, one thinks perforce, and first of all, of her personages, men and women—Silas, Adam, Hetty, Mrs. Poyser, Maggie and her brother, Dorothea and Causabon, Tito, Deronda. Such other valuable adjuncts as situation, description, style, come in for subsequent appreciation; but it is this great woman's characters who arise as witnesses to her art and her genius. George Eliot's earlier training in the ways of scholarship and her inherent proneness to psychologic philosophizing could not, in the morning blush of literary creation, quench her native gift for characterization. Nor, however much the former encroached upon the latter, was the gift ever disastrously obscured until the evening day of "Theophrastus Such." The tendency was dangerous, even for a nature of her calibre: with a lesser writer it is sure to make trouble. We are observing to-day how Mrs. Humphrey Ward gains in the power of characterization and, in fact, in all ways as an artist, by so much as she eschews definite, dogmatic purpose. The parallel is especially interesting, because in some prime requisites—in seriousness, in breadth of view, in largeness and nobility of spirit—Mrs. Ward, more than any other current fictionist, represents the elder woman. In the author of "Marcella" the loss of variety and strength of character-making, although in part a personal matter, is due in some measure to the change that has come over our literary ideals.

This fact, that the novelist stands or falls by characterization, has its interesting application when we come to look at later novel-making. It explains the relatively limited appeal of leaders cried up by critics whose admiration for construction, description, and style make them forget the preëminent thing. Of course, we must grant that the perfect novel—like the perfect man, a purely hypothetical creature—will have all the qualities in due proportion: fresh invention, masterful development, characters that live and move and have their being, description full of picturesqueness and power, all conveyed in a diction that of itself means literature. But, humanly speaking, this is the unattainable ideal or, at least, the unattained. Conceding this much, it may be stated boldly that where the present-day fictionist fails

above all else is in character—the sign, par excellence, of the creator. A few years ago it would have been in consonance with the facts to say that he was weak in invention as well. But now, with romances appearing daily, and startling plots in the very air one breathes, this lack is less felt. But character-making, yes. Nor can the blame justly be laid on the public, which is always eager to welcome a piece of veritable character-limning.

As I write, "David Harum" is the best selling story—and therefore book, since fiction still has a corner on literature. Why is this? Because it contains one thoroughly racy and enjoyable character; the rest is naught. The book is not a novel. It has no plot worth mentioning, and but little construction; being a purely conventional treatment of the love-motif. The nominal hero's only mortal use is, that Uncle David may have some one to talk to steadily. But the tale has a bona fide creation in David himself; and this is enough to give it a remarkable and deserved popularity. Yet reflect a moment that there is not even a second-rate novel by Dickens which does not contain, I will not say one, but half a dozen, humorous character-types, any one of which might be named as an offset to the shrewd, kindly horse-trader and country banker. This is not said in the spirit of detraction, but merely to bring home the thought that we have fallen on a paucity of real character-creation, which results in an almost pathetically cordial reception for it when a modicum of it is proffered.

Nor is it Jingoism, by the way, to remark that the introduction of some of the Southern and Western types so saliently depicted by younger American novelists—Page and Harris, Stuart, Thanet, Wister, Garland, Chopin, Fernald, and others—is as hopeful a sign as current fiction can show, and one hardly to be paralleled in England. In the earlier days Bret Harte took a unique place because of this same power, albeit not always used aright. Who, let us inquire, are the living personages in the stories of Henry James? Verily, since the days of "The American," the best in this kind are but shadows. Stevenson, admirable in the other cardinal points of invention, construction, and a style that sets him apart from his contemporaries, has also thrown out upon the fictional canvas a few figures which are distinct —Alan Breck, David Balfour, both the Ballantraes, Kirstie the elder, and quite a portrait-gallery of rascals the most firm-bodied and picturesque in the novel-writing of our time.

Can as much be said for Kipling? Very strong he is, of a truth, in invention, construction, description, and dialogue; but where are his characters? Outside of Mowgli and the Soldiers Three, has he given us any? An obvious answer is, that being primarily a short-story maker, he is, by the definition of his art, excluded from triumphs in this kind, since characterization requires a larger canvas. There is something in this; but it does not affect the main proposition that Kipling's forte, thus far, has not been the delineation of personality. That he has been able, within short-story limits, to stamp Mulvaney and his commensals with so much individuality speaks volumes for his natural abilities in a perilous endeavor. Nevertheless, having in view the number of his volumes and the striking effects he has produced, it is worth noting that Kipling's contribution to fictional portraiture has not been large.

It is curious, and a bit amusing, to see how current novels are heralded with trumpets of prophecy and followed by columnar eulogies, when, in this article of character truly alive, they are *nil*. An example of this class—not a small one—just now is Theodore Watts Dunton's "Aylwin." Undoubtedly, the story has romantic poetry in it of a strained, fantastic, and morbid kind. But, in respect of characterization, surely it is a failure. Revert in memory to such a humdrum realist as Anthony Trollope, in order vividly to realize why that fiction-maker, whose class is confessedly not the first, is likely to keep his place in the suffrages of a large, and not undistinguished, constituency. The folk of the "Barchester Chronicles" may be commonplace and unexciting; but they are verifiable and cling to the mind.

This clear bodying forth of men and women in

the novel sets up so good a claim to attention
that it will often cover a multitude of sins. And
it really seems as if, with the rapidly increasing
skill in the other technical points of novelistic
art, this potent, this supreme power of characterization were in danger of its life. Is it that our
story-tellers lack gift, genius, or simply that, in
the care spent upon analysis or construction, description or style, or all of them, they have lost
sight of the most vital element in any and all
fiction? Or is it again—very plausible this—that
problem and principle have led our fictionists
somewhat away from the straight-away actions of
flesh-and-blood folk? The pessimist will incline
toward the easy solution, concluding that it is all
a question of ability; that we have fallen on little
days, if not evil; that when the gods go, the half-
gods arrive. Genius was of yore: now is the
time of carefully cultivated talents. But the student of social history, and literature in its relation thereto, will prefer to see in the wonderful
development of the art of fiction during the last
quarter-century a more essential cause for the
temporary abeyance in the power of creating
salient, unforgettable characters. I say "temporary," as expressing the belief that, just as we have
witnessed a distinct reaction from the plotless tale
of psychologic analysis toward stories of incident
and action, so we are likely to see a return to the
old emphasis on character.

The folk of fiction in the future will not be so

much pegs to hang theories upon, as human beings to associate with, to laugh and cry with, and to part from right unwillingly. And they will be more wholesome company withal than they have been, as a rule, of late. Novelists must so realize their characters that the bidding them good-bye means pain and loss to the writers themselves—as Dickens walked the streets of Paris the best part of one night in utter misery because little Paul Dombey had fallen on final sleep; or as Daudet was overcome when he had similar experience with his lad of the imagination, the Piteous Jack. The inexorable corollary to such feeling on the side of the creator is an affectionate faith in those characters on the side of the world of novel-readers. Let this not be forgotten in a day of the deification of technic and of an overweening desire to handicap the personages of fiction by making them more or less colorless exponents of a principle, a class, or a theory.

By the knowing novelist of to-day the exposure of himself as caring vitally whether his manikins live or die is something to be avoided—even sneered at in others. Such an attitude is declared to be naïve, inartistic. This is an ominous sign. Charles Reade, weeping over the parting with "Peg Woffington"—"my darling," he called her— is a far more convincing spectacle to a host of honest-hearted readers, than is that of Thackeray at the end of the "Newcomes" ringing down the curtain and putting his puppets in the box—in other words, smashing all the illusion of the tale by announcing in the first person its fictive nature. The cold, aloof position of the late-century fiction-maker toward the people of his brain and heart may be high art, but it is precious poor humanity. And it is this perhaps more than any other one thing that is likely to keep out of our fiction the red blood of life. "But," cries the novelist, "look at my skill, my ingenuity, my technical excellences in half a dozen particulars of a difficult art." To which the public replies: "True, it is magnificent, but it is not war."

THE CULT OF THE HISTORICAL ROMANCE.

There is much to justify the remark that literature, like life, has its ephemeral fashions. A long yesterday ago, the epic was the favorite form of narration; later, the drama ruled; to-day, the novel is supreme. And within the limits marked out for that wide term, fiction, the variations in the kind of story are so many and apparently so arbitrary that they may seem, on a superficial glance, to depend upon incalculable social whims and vagaries. Indeed, we may go further and concede to this view, that, from decade to decade, certain elements of fashion do influence literary matters with the result that, in the case of an author (and the same is true of a literary form), he attracts a following, only to be set aside ere long for some newer interest. Nevertheless, the idea that fashion controls literature, as it does woman's dress, for example, is one based upon specious appearances; it ignores underlying causes which, in reality, define literary evolution.

Psychologic laws and sociologic conditions explain shifts of taste which, superficially considered, seem as unpredicable as the desire of a coquette. Thus, taking the literary forms just mentioned, a certain stage of civilization demands that its stories be poured into the majestic mold of the epic; an age more sophisticate, with a keener sense of national life and a greater solidarity, possessing what may be called a practical bias for action, favors the play; while our own time, with its tremendously complex social needs and interrelations, finds in prose fiction, so flexible in form, so all-embracing in theme, its natural outlet of expression. This single fact, that our day has elected the novel as its representative form, may be regarded in two ways; it may be taken simply as a sign of the shallowness and lightheadedness of these latter years, an indication of degeneracy, or it may be studied as revelatory of the aims and ideals of the time, and hence full of interesting suggestions. The former is the conclusion of the unthinking hasty; the latter, that of the scholar.

But, now, what is true of the different forms, is true of fiction in its several sorts. Plainly marked changes have taken place during the past century (to go no further back) with a comparative regularity which a glance at literary history will make apparent.

Scott, by right of power, introduced the modern historical romance. He stamped this kind with the seal of his genius, although romanticism in the novel was living no feeble life before him. In fact, the story of romantic quality was creeping and spreading like a prairie fire all along the second half of the eighteenth century, but we do

not feel its heat until the genial influence of the
Waverley Master. This romantic impulse and
direction had by the year 1850 become a thing
obsolete and only sporadically cultivated. G. P.
R. James, whose array of Christian names has the
effect of suggesting the too leisurely movement of
his many romances, did more than his share, perhaps, in checking the taste for this kind of story-
writing. By the middle century Dickens and
Thackeray had returned to the method of Richardson and Fielding and Smollett; the novel of
analysis, depicting contemporary manners and
types, was again in full vogue. This counter-
swing of the pendulum brought on the noteworthy
development conveniently (though misleadingly)
summarized under the familiar term "realism."
With this extension of the fictionist's field, came
an increased desire for accuracy and what is called
truth; and too often this truth was of the exclusively factual sort, that which deals with visible
phenomena or with scientific laws; or worse, it
came to mean an insistence upon the grosser de-
tails of the life sensual. This instinct for particularity and verity had, however, its legitimate manifestations, and did great service in rubbing
bright the mirror of the novel, so that it might
reflect without distortion the image of the time.
The importance as well as dominance of the so-
called realistic movement during the past five-and-
twenty years can hardly be overrated. The critic
cannot quarrel with the statement that it repre-

sents fiction's most characteristic evolution in the
century's last quarter. What other tendency has
been so widespread and influential—the influence
amounting to a revolution of method, aim, and
interpretation?

Yet the very insistence upon analysis and detail
self-doomed it to suffer a reaction. The romantic
revival of the past decade draws attention to the
inevitable swing-back of the pendulum, a movement away from the realistic and towards the romantic, and freshly emphasizes for the scholar
the laws by which fiction in its historic growth
shifts from one to the other of these two main
purposes. Keeping to the figure of the pendulum,
we might say that the arc described has for its
two limits, realism, the desire for truth, and romanticism, the desire for poetry. Quite as truly
as in the physical world, a swing one way implies
a swing the other, and corresponding to the
central pull of gravity is that same instinct of
normal human nature, drawing the novel back to
a middle point of art. Thus, in a sense, scientific
laws of ebb and flow control the changes in this
typical modern literary form. And hence the
present marked popularity of romantic narrative
is a phase which one with his eye on the evolution
of fiction since Scott could have predicated with
little trouble.

Our opinion of the momentary cult of the romance will be modified in the first place by our
attitude towards the romantic as a method, and

in the last by our estimate of the quality of the
work at present being done under that banner-cry.
As to the former, it seems fair to say that if by romance we mean the truthful handling of the more
exceptional and noble incidents and characters in
life, in such wise as not to imply that they are
more frequent in occurrence than in reality they
are, the romantic is a welcome visitor. Certainly
it is inspiring to meet people in fiction who ex-
emplify the finer traits of humanity, and to be
introduced to situations which stir the soul out
of the walking trance of everyday existence. Nor
is there any harm in it, along with the good, unless life and the folk thereof are treated with a
certain sickly pseudo-idealism which makes the
world an impossible phantasmagoria, and its men
and women to appear like the philosopher's trees
walking. To condemn that sort of fictional narcotic is not to condemn the true romance: *ab
abusu ad usum non valet consequentia.* The critic
may well cry up the nobler order of romance
which includes the right kind of realism, because
it tells the truth about the most interesting and
uplifting aspects of human life, while it does not
fall into the error of putting too much stress upon
the lower stages of the slow painful process by
which man mounts to higher things.

But now as to the product itself, which in these
latter days is put out so generously, stamped with
the promiseful trade-mark, Romanticism. That
there is much good in it, only the confirmed cynic

will deny. Three roads it takes; that of the pastoral idyl, that of the modern adventure-tale, and that of the historical romance. And the most notable results just now seem to come by this last-named way. In England the young romantics led by Stevenson, with such doughty lieutenants as Doyle, Hope, Weyman, Barrie and Quiller-Couch, with later writers of whom Hewlett is typical, come to mind. To these and others of their faith the "fair field of old romance" has been attractive and yielded golden fruit in two senses—the artistic and the mercantile. Stimulated by their example, American writers have waked up to a realization of the rich historic material native to their own land; and major attempts like Dr. Mitchell's "Hugh Wynne," Mr. Stimson's "King Noanett," Mr. Allen's "The Choir Invisible" and "The Reign of Law," Mr. Churchill's "Richard Carvel," Mr. Ford's "Janice Meredith," Miss Jewett's "A Tory Lover," and Miss Johnston's "To Have and to Hold," are only a few among a less conspicuous many.

Most of these books are welcome both as a contribution to native history and as an extension of the individual outlook upon life; they have sufficient art, truth and power to justify their appearance. The warmth of their reception, indeed, while it may be explained in part by saying that the public, starved for years, was ahungered for imaginative presentation of any sort, means quite as truly that such like novels have genuine merit. The suc-

cesses of the moment are mostly in this line; not
exclusively—witness the merry sale of "David
Harum,"—but so prevailingly that the phrase, a
romantic cult, as applied to the present situation,
is not inaccurately descriptive.

And the inevitable result is at hand. Second-
rate writers are turning to the historic romance,
not because they are compelled from within to do
so, but rather because they strive to meet an
obvious demand; their impulse is mercantile, not
artistic. The market is in danger of being flooded
with spurious imitations of the real article. Not
a few fiction-fashioners are serving not Scott but
Mammon. Several current stories are far from
being finished works of art, nor indeed do they
show sufficient power or skill, one would suppose,
to justify their vogue; yet how wide an audience
have they found! Such diet cannot be peptonic
in the long run; its careless acceptance will speed
the day of the return of an exaggerated realism.
It is hardly too much to say that in the present
year of grace the general public is fairly rabid for
heroic stories of the past. Publishers are suggesting historic themes to novelists, who, on their side,
are grubbing in old records and furbishing up
their memories of bygone centuries and countries.
Booksellers buy their wares, keenly cognizant of
this popular appeal. The proprietor of the leading book-shop in a large Western city was filling
his front window one morning with Ford's "Janice
Meredith," just then hot from the press; and upon

my expressing a mild doubt as to his getting rid
of so many copies, replied briskly that the more
probable trouble would be to keep the story in
stock.   This was not faith without works, to be
sure, for Mr. Ford is a popular novelist; but the
fact that the book in question was an historic romance, and of American motive at that, furnished
the extra weight to turn the scales.   Had the fiction been of the more psychologic sort my book-
seller's voice had not sounded with such a chirrup
of confidence.   And in justification of his judgment, in the first week's sale thirteen thousand
copies of the book went off, and its subsequent
fortune has been of like kind.

Now one may admire the historical romance in
its place and degree, and yet deprecate the tendency to laud romance for romance's sake.   For this
last attitude brings about the circulation of much
that is mediocre, if not worthless; it holds back
the true development of fictional art; it tends to
a partizan patronage of the part rather than the
whole; and, as already hinted, it is very likely to
precipitate a reactionary devotion to the narrow
realism from which there would seem to be a
happy escape.   One's very dislike of this stupid,
vulgar abuse of fiction inclines one to cry a halt
on the present uncritical deification of the so-
called romantic.   Nor, frankly, does the romance
give the full picture.   To lay the scenes of a novel
in older times is no warrant that it will be either
artistic or readable.

From the very nature of the historical romance
the danger of missing the right method is
peculiarly strong. An effective romance must
possess, over and above its verisimilitude, the reproduction of bygone speech, manners, and character types, those elemental human qualities
which shall make it interesting, expressive. This
quality it is which gives Scott earlier and Sien-
kiewicz later a claim upon the world of readers,
critical and general. To secure this result has, I
say, difficulties exceptional and only to be overcome by a life-work. To appeal through
piquancy of costuming or the unhackneyed nature
of the situations is legitimate enough; but this is
subordinate to that essential humanity in a romance which forces the thoughtful to call it finely
representative.

While I cannot go so far as Professor Brander
Matthews, who believes that it is this alone which
makes the historical story survive its own day,
the local color and the illusion of the past being
largely unknown, since no man really knows a
former century, I do agree with him heartily in
the primary necessity that fiction of this sort shall
show the abiding interests and passions. Pan
Michel may be honestly Slavonic as to type, but
it is the more important fact that he is a child-
hearted lover and hero-patriot which brings all
nations to his death-scene. Mr. Frederick Har-
rison, himself a historian, concedes to the writer
of historical romance the opportunity of what he

calls "historic realism," a phrase he uses in regard to "Richard Yea and Nay." It would seem
true that, in a sense, the very perfection of the
illusion in a picture of past times constitutes its
claim to realism—a reality which neither reader
nor writer can ever prove at first hand nor even
by documentary evidence.

A further thought forces itself upon us here.
Romantic literature, to be honest, must stand for
the romantic spirit of the age that produces it;
otherwise it is felt to be *pastiche,* an imitation,
not a reality. Is our age, in truth, one that finds
its deepest, most sympathetic expression in the
historical novel? On the contrary, is it not the
strong, fine, truthful representation of present-
day vital issues which most appeals to the largest
number of educated readers? The question may
at least be asked. If so it is, then the current
craze for the romance has no firm rootage, and
another reason for its probable brief cultivation is
found. Prof. W. P. Trent, in a recent suggestive
paper, goes so far as to say that "there is no
genuine spirit of romanticism abroad to-day;"
which is a more sweeping assertion than those of
us who believe that the interest in romance is in a
sense eternal would care to make. Nevertheless,
it may be argued with much show of reason that
the modern attitude of mind after a half century
of science, expressed in the august word Evolution,
and after so thorough an indoctrination in the
idea that the novel's chief business is to depict life

as it is, for our instruction, cannot quite go back
to the old dissipation in the not seldom noxious
sweets of romantic illusion or delusion.

Certain evils, then, are possible to the enthusiasm for historic romance, and it is perhaps as
well to draw attention to them just at the point
when, in the "first fine careless rapture" of appreciation, the critical faculty may be lulled to
sleep. Let us have the romance of the larger,
nobler kind, by all means; but let us sternly refuse to read history fiction that is neither sound
history nor good fiction. In our relish for the
(perfectly admissible) presentation of heroics
(within limits which should be definitely understood), let us not overlook the admirable work
steadily being done in the United States, as elsewhere, in the vast and varied fields of sane realism. If we would not witness a woful return to
realism of the baser sort, we must take care not to
get a surfeit even of a good thing. The teaching
of literary history here is so plain that he who
runs may read.

The present taste for romance, natural and
wholesome as it is, does not necessarily mean a
permanent triumph of that particular tendency;
in fact, to believe it did, were to make light of the
lesson taught by the historic life of fiction since
the year 1814, when the Waverley Novels began to
bewitch the imaginations of men. Just because of
the vigor of its romantic impulse will the pendulum swing back toward realism; and it lies

primarily with the intelligent reading public whether the counter movement is not excessive, producing once again in current novels the petty particularity, the dreary lack of incident, the attention to malodorous material, and the waspish interpretation of life, which, in various combinations, are associated in many minds with the hard-ridden word, realism.

THE LOVE MOTIVE IN MODERN
FICTION

It may be said that of old a story in fiction of the English tongue meant a love story. This is a generalization that the memories of novel readers of an elder generation will justify. As love is the central fact and solar force in the life of man as he emerges from the brute; so, naturally, it was given the role of protagonist in the human passion play. "Love," says Mr. Howells in a recent piece of fiction, "has to be in every picture of life, as it has to be in every life."

Peter Bayne, in 1860, defined the novel as a "domestic history" in which the incidents and evolution centered in the amatory passion. Even present day dictionaries emphasize the love theme, in describing fiction. In the fiction of the eighteenth century the love depicted was, take it by and large, stilted, narrow and unideal. But it played a very important rôle, nevertheless, whether it was handled in its coarser manifestations by a Fielding or treated with the comparatively prim propriety of a Jane Austen.

The novel, then, of all present literary forms most reflective of modern society, has mirrored the thoughts, feelings and acts connected with love to the exclusion, or, at least, to the comparative

31

neglect, of other social motor forces. But in the remarkable development of fiction which has taken place during the past quarter-century—a movement beginning to crystallize into definite results with Zola at the time of the Franco-Prussian war, a change is to be chronicled in the handling and valuation of the love-motive and its successive stages. The result has suggestion and interest not only for its bearings on modern fiction but also on the life such literature portrays.

In the treatment of love in the old-fashioned "goody-goody" story of English manufacture earlier in our century, that passion was regarded as fitly interpreted by two young folk of opposite sex in the pre-nuptial period; under proper social restrictions they met, were attracted, wooing and winning followed in due course and the novelist's duty was done when he had effected a happy culmination at the altar—a word to which the later, more cynical exponent of fiction prefixes the letter h. "And so they were married and lived happily forever after," is the fairy-tale phrase dropping the curtain upon this tame dénouement. I am aware that this is a sweeping statement, that older English fiction sometimes treats the love motive more robustly. The amatory relations of Mr. B. and Pamela, the gallantries of Tom Jones appear vigorous and sufficiently unconventional when set over against these milk-and-water episodes. But the run of stories prior to the incoming of realism was of the sort indicated; the ex-

perience of veteran novel readers will sustain me.
The foreign novelists and critics made fun of the
English for this tendency.

Gradually, however, and no doubt under foreign
influence, came a bolder handling, a wider extension of the theme. Love began to be recognized
as an explosive capable of tearing people to pieces;
a power productive of unhappiness along with
felicity. Shakespeare's "The course of true love
never did run smooth," became a motto for tales
in which many obstacles to the eventual pleasant
round-up in church were imagined, and men and
maidens not only loved, but misunderstood, quar-
reled, and lost or went astray. These narratives
were more or less sad, but not necessarily pessi-
mistic; they marked a step away from the stereo-
typed "good ending" of the primitive love-tale.
But sentimental they were to the lachrymosal pitch
of a Mackenzie. And they testify to a broaden-
ing conception of life in one of its most vital aspects; life as compounded of bitter and sweet in
uncertain shifting proportions, and not as con-
tinuously saccharine. This sad ending became in
time as conventional as the earlier happy ending.
The ladies who wept over Richardson's "Clarissa
Harlowe" and knelt imploring the novelist to spare
their beloved heroine's life, were evidently less
inured to fictional pain than their novel-reading
descendants.

Then came another extension of subject. It
occurred to those who narrate imagined deeds that

to stop at marriage was unfair and absurd; an
arbitrary halt at a mid-station of the life journey,
when stirring haps and mishaps lay beyond. So,
with the French as leaders, enters the whole brood
of fiction dealing with marital relations and an-
swerable for so much that is malodorous, but also
for a great deal that is strong and fine. Here such
names as Hardy, Meredith and Moore, Tolstoy,
Flaubert, Zola and Daudet, Sudermann and
Björnson, D'Annunzio, Valera and Bazan, come
to mind as representative, standing for many
others. Main attention came to be given to post-
marital experiences. The novelists were fain to
illustrate the homely saying, "When a man mar-
ries his trouble begins," and the miseries of the
mismated were set forth in epic sweep. And by
an inevitable farther step, the relations of im-
propriety—the French *"drame à trois"*—have been
delineated with a gusto and particularity which
have left little to be hoped for,—or dreaded.

It is as natural for George Meredith or Thomas
Hardy or George Moore to show the tragedies of
unconventional sex relations as it was for Dickens
to sum up those of the oppressed poor or Thackeray to describe family embroglios. Thus, in a
progressive treatment of love happy, love unhappy, love sensual and love of the *union libre*
type, the later novelists, outside of our language
most noticeably, but within it to an appreciable
degree, have moved away from the quaint and
comfortable depictment of the pretty boy-and-girl

sentiment, to do justice to an imperious, untrammeled passion in the full exercise of its tragic power. They have now run the gamut, it would seem; love as a social force has been sounded in its complete diapason. Tolstoy's "Anna Karénina," beginning the narrative where the old-fashioned tale would have closed, and conducting an unhappy marriage situation through an experience of guilty love to a tragic conclusion, is typical of the class.

Hence has followed a shift in the use of this motive in fiction, which I would emphasize. It would appear that novelists, by an unconscious reaction, perhaps, or it may be with the feeling that even a theme so central and dominant as this, can be overworked, have, for the time at least, relegated love to a place nearer the circumference of the circle and for the nonce are finding their stimulus elsewhere. A plain sign of this is the recrudescence of the story of adventure. Fighting instead of loving, furnishes the attraction, and plot takes the place of esoteric emotion. During the past dozen years the tale of objective incident and action in English fiction has all but pre-empted the field; a significant change of theme, indeed. To be sure, love is often admitted into these narratives, but the point is that as a motive it is subsidiary to the major appeal. A striking example is given us in the work of the two writers of English fiction confessedly leaders in contemporary literature. I refer to Stevenson and Kipling.

Neither of them has awarded to love the old-time, traditional post of honor.

It has been said commonly of Stevenson that he could not manage love as a theme. He himself in the ever delightful Letters confesses with dangerous frankness his lack of confidence in handling this motive. He felt that his power lay elsewhere. Nevertheless, he was in his latest work coming to admit this more lyric interest, along with the heroic; "Kidnapped" and its sequel, "David Balfour," are an instructive contrast in this regard. While the former is a straightaway adventure tale, with scant attention to petticoats, the other, written some years later, contains a charming heroine and some of the prettiest lovemaking in modern fiction. Nor will the true Stevenson lover ever forget "Prince Otto," an earlier work that deals with the love motive in a charming vein of delicate, quaint poetry. In Stevenson's final books, too, "St. Ives" and "Weir of Hermiston," this interest is more prominent. "St. Ives," indeed, is a story in which adventure and sweethearting run hand in hand; and that fascinating torso "Weir," so far as it goes, might fairly be called a love-tale, though Mr. Colvin's postscript shows us that the objective incident of peril and derring-do was to have culminating force. Stevenson, in a word, might be characterized as a writer who as he matured was led more and more to a consideration of the eternal feminine. Yet his genius did not find its most authentic inspiration there; and looking to the full range of his imaginative creation, it may be declared that he used the love motive but charily; his main business was with the other passions of men.

With Kipling the thesis receives still more obvious illustration. In the comparatively slight, tentative sketches known as the Gadsby series, he attempted the treatment of amatory affairs after the manner of the cynic. But that sort of thing ill suited his vigorous grasp of life and healthy sanity, and was soon sloughed off. The bulk of the Indian Tales—and the best of them—, the later volumes of short stories whose themes are not of the East; the wonderful "Jungle Books;" the collaborated "Naulahka;" and the capital sea-yarn "Captains Courageous," all of these find their intensity of interest outside love. The later collections of short tales, "Many Inventions" and "The Day's Work," do not violate my statement. "The Brushwood Boy" in the second named volume, a story in which the love passion is certainly central, stands out in contrast with the rest of the narratives. An exception may be made of "The Light That Failed," where obviously the relations of Dick and Maisie claim our chief attention, although if we examine the book for its purpose, it will appear that the study of the artist temperament is the author's main aim. Still, this fiction may fairly enough be called a love story. But for a writer of a dozen volumes, Kipling has indicated distinctly his preference for other motives.

No one in thinking of either him or Stevenson would dream of citing them as exponents of the so-called master-passion.

The same tendency is to be seen in the work of the one contemporary woman writer whose fiction has the scope, poise, dignity and art likely to give her more than ephemeral distinction. Mrs. Humphrey Ward has not ignored the love motive, but rather has made it subordinate to other interests,—religion, politics, sociology. Her early book, "Miss Bretherton," might be described as a love tale, pure and simple. But with and since "Robert Elsmere" her vision has been wider. The affectional relations of the sexes are dealt with in that novel also, of course; as likewise, in some phases of its multiform power, in "David Grieve," in "Marcella," in "Sir George Tressady," "The Story of Bessie Costrell," "Helbeck of Bannisdale," and especially in "Eleanor." But, with the exception of "Eleanor," none of them are love stories in the conventional sense. Even in "Eleanor," which would properly enough, I suppose, be termed a love tale, the interest is in the sharply contrasted women characters far more than in the outcome of Bannisty's somewhat febrile passion. What the reader is likely to recall first in these books of Mrs. Ward is the modern clergyman confronted with doubt; the aspiring young woman learning by dint of hard experience the true difficulties between the classes and masses; the humble born man fighting his way to the spiritual peace that comes out of emo-

tional storm and stress; the great lady influential
in affairs, a power behind the throne; the peasant
girl crushed by her pitiless environment; the well-
born mine owner anxious to adjust the questions of
labor versus capital and solving the problem with
his knife; the agnostic girl and Romanist aristocrat trying to make love overleap the barriers of
environment and temperament. All through these
well wrought and noble volumes woman walks as
meet mate to man, shoulder to shoulder with him
in the struggle. Indeed, Mrs. Ward and Meredith are conspicuous among present day novelists
of repute and power in delineating the New Woman in the high sense of the contemned word;
which is to say, the Eternal Woman under the
broader, more exacting conditions of our complex
social life. George Meredith's Diana is a creation
only possible to this new conception of woman.
Indeed, it is instructive to compare Meredith's
Lucy in "The Ordeal of Richard Feveril," a book
published over forty years ago, with so late a
woman characterization as his Diana; it suggests
that the novelist himself changes with the time.
In the same way, food for reflection can be found
in a comparison of George Eliot and Mrs. Ward in
their respective treatments of women. A veritable
evolution of view can be traced.

The rejuvenescence of romance which has been so
noticeable in England and America within the past
half dozen years, and the revival of the historical
novel both there and in the United States, also

stand for a mood which, while it does not necessarily exclude the treatment of love, at least looks
more naturally to objective incident and bellicose
action for its subject-material. It may then fairly
be postulated from present indications that the
love theme, traditionally so central, and illuminating the course of English fiction from Fielding to
Meredith will be in the future—not eliminated—
but handled in conjunction with and subordinate
to the modern interests which have so vastly ex-
tended the content of the novel in our time. Or
is it saner prophecy to declare that, by a natural
law of reaction, the novelists of the next century
will come back to an older assumption, reinstating
the love that is after all the light of life, in its
old time queenship? One consideration makes
this dubious. The shifted place of the love motive
is due to the shifted place of woman in the social
complex. She is no longer reared to regard marriage as a sole vocation. The daughters of well-
to-do and cultured folk are not infrequently educated nowadays with an eye to self-supporting
work. Even if parental encouragement lacks,
modern girls in increasing numbers are ambitious
to achieve in some field of endeavor. The spinster
of to-day no longer sits with folded hands by the
lonesome hearth sadly reminiscent, knitting her
employ, regret her mood. She turns artist, house-
decorator, architect, teacher, actor, musician,
nurse, writer, physician or lawyer. She looks to
the future, not to the past. With this infinitely

more complex activity and its correspondent
breadth of outlook, it is easy to understand that
the conventional value of love to her life—" 'Tis
woman's whole existence," quoth Byron—should
give way; and equally easy to understand that
story makers, perceiving the social drift, should
register it in their feignings of human intercourse.
The term "old maid" is fast passing, at least in
any opprobrious sense. Balzac did a daring thing
in making the woman of thirty interesting and
eligible for a prominent position in his fiction.
It is now the commonplace of novel-writing
to show her power, her charm, her right to a useful life independent of the poor creature, man.
Dickens's women, as a rule, seem old-fashioned to
us as we read him to-day; his presentation of
them in this respect is one of the chief explana-
tions of the fact.

It must be remembered, too, in the discussion
that the representation of love varies with nation-
ality. The tendency in English fiction to remove
this motive from its supreme position is by no
means typical of the European literatures. The
Latin races, as a whole, for example, incline still
to make fictional interest dependent upon love,
and usually upon love sensual. Mrs. Crawford,
writing in the lamented Cosmopolis of the brilliant
young Italian, D'Annunzio, remarks that in his
country the love motive predominates to an extent
that sober Northern natures cannot realize. Of
Spain, this is also true, though to a less degree.

In France, however, a land always sensitively in the van of intellectual and social progress, the prevalence of the novel of passion is by no means what it was a few years ago. Zola's latest novels subordinate the love motive; witness the trilogy of the cities.

It is, then, in fiction of our own tongue that the revolt from the tyranny of love as an all-absorbing theme can be traced most convincingly. And it seems to me that this is a testimonial to the inspiring breadth and variety of our novel. Sneers have been plenty in respect to the narrow prudery of the life-view expressed in English novels; but unwillingness to treat of the bestial aspects of love is no whit narrower than unwillingness to admit the other main interests and passions of mankind. In this admission our fiction leads, and, so far as it goes, such leadership is a proof, not of narrowness, but of breadth,—of a truer insight and a finer sense of proportion in looking out upon the great human show.

Still, let us admit that the somewhat remarkable change I have glanced at is really not so much the disappearance of Love, as an altered (and broader) conception of it, together with the admission of other interests as the life picture has grown larger. Disappear love never will from fiction until it does from Life,—which will happen only when our sun has become a moon. Sex love in the latest and noblest conception is one phase, and a precious phase, of the all-love,—a power and a principle of many manifestations; friend-love, child-love, parent-love, patriotism, nature-love, love for truth, for religion,—an idea finely brought out in an essay by Sidney Lanier posthumously published. It is natural that with this broader apperception of the word, novelists should elect not only these more varied phases of Love, but also use war, politics, socialism, social ambitions, trade, sports, art, literature, religion, as motives to make their pages animated and cheerful and more truly representative of Life itself.

THE DARK IN LITERATURE

Those who are sensitive to literature at all turn to it for various reasons,—for rest, pleasure, comfort, instruction, uplift. To forget its power to make this manifold appeal were sadly to restrict its influence. Literature follows the gospel injunction; it is many things to many men. This, indeed, is only a roundabout way of saying that it is a great force in the world; for how otherwise could it get a wide hearing?

Nevertheless, I am persuaded that the larger number of readers still look, as they have always looked, to poem and essay, play and story — to belles lettres, in short — for what may be called pleasure. Of old, this was overwhelmingly true; it is somewhat less apparent now, when both author and reader have come to take their literature seriously, and duty at times crowds delight to the wall. However, the wayfaring man continues to insist, in good set terms, on an agreeable time when he opens a book; and if you are fain to instruct him you must do it cautiously without overmuch announcement of your laudable purpose. Unless the pill be sugar-coated he will have none of it; homœopathy is the school he favors.

Critics who overlook this natural human tendency are letting themselves get professional and out of touch with their fellow mortals. I believe that, while our conception of the use of literature may well be a broader one, this pathetic desire of average humanity to be pleased is a wholesome notification to critic and creator, to special student and him of the inner circle, that the main business of letters is to furnish joy to the children of men. Especially is this thought pertinent to-day, when the other obligations of literature are underscored.

It is as well to remember that unhappiness is not an end in itself. The assumption, by the way, that a book must either please or instruct, as if the two demands were mutually exclusive, is absurd—an example of false logic. Rather may it be said, as Stevenson has it, that "to please is to serve; and so far from its being difficult to instruct while you amuse, it is difficult to do the one thoroughly without the other."

But no honest person can go far in the fruitful study of the masterpieces of thought and expression without coming face to face with the need of extending this pleasure-giving concept of literature, or, at any rate, of using the word pleasure in a fuller significance. He finds that it is very much with literature as it is with the weather. All sorts are encountered, the stormy with the bland; and even in the presumably serene climate of the so-called immortals, halcyon days by no means run the year round. He is confronted, sooner or later, with the questions: How broad may I make my definition of this elusive term pleasure? What is the proper proportion of light and shade in these pictures of life painted with words instead of colors? Has the dark—meaning thereby the somber and sad, the terrible, brutal, and abnormal elements of life reflected in books— any justification? And where are the bounds to be set? Upon the answers depend his whole attitude toward literature and the amount of substantive enrichment received from it. I know of no more important moment in personal literary culture than the one of this decision; and it was with a sense of this importance that my theme was chosen.

Few even of those who are unfriendly to the dark in literature, will deny that the sad has some right there, or that pleasure may co-exist with sadness. To shut out the imaginative presentation of the tragic would result in a woful weakening and crippling of literature—would, indeed, decapitate masterpiece after masterpiece. From the time that Aristotle pointed out the noble function of tragedy in purging our souls through terror and pity, the major creators in literature have steadily illustrated his position. And, in truth, long before the great Greek critic, the Hebrew rhapsodists shook their time, and after-time, with the very thunders of Sinai. It might also be said that the precious places, the mighty effects, in world-literature, are just those where the grave things of life are set before us surcharged with passion, but touched with beauty, set to consoling music, and illumined by imperishable hopes. **Job,** superbly alone and afflicted on his ash-heap; Antigone, going smiling to her tomb; Chaucer's Griselda, patient and amazed at her ill treatment, and exclaiming, as the thought of her husband's earlier love for her overwhelmed her mind:

> "O gode God! how gentil and how kinde
> Ye semed by your speche and your visage
> The day that makéd was our mariage";

Lear appealing to the stormy heavens, since they were old like him; Dante listening to Francesca's piteous tale of love, strong though in hell; Gretchen in the Garden, conscious of her guilt, yet crying with that infinitely pathetic child-cry:

> "Yet, everything that led me here
> Was oh, so good, was oh, so dear";

Beatrice Cenci, talking of her hair just before she goes out to the block; Mildred, in Browning's "A Blot in the 'Scutcheon," with those wonderful girlish words of hers:

> "I—I was so young!
> Beside, I loved him, Thorold—and I had
> No mother; God forgot me: so I fell "—

these, I say, are the scenes that to the lover of literature rise up in memory like southern stars in the night heavens, stars whose sombre setting is the very condition of the splendor of their shining. Give us this kind of sadness, by all means, for by it our souls grow and we are made to feel the sacred majesty of humankind. It is not so much sadness, strictly speaking, that we experience in looking at these moving life dramas, as a sort of sober joy. Our sense of *homo sapiens* is enlarged as to his essential dignity and worth. This is sadness, not for its own sake, but for humanity's.

Nor should we forget that, besides this proper acceptance of what I may term the legitimate and wholesome sad in literature, many folk have a morbid love of sadness for its own sake. There is no hypochondriac like your young person in the storm and stress period of his career. Fears are his food and tears his daily portion. In youth we like to take our pleasures sadly; while in the years that bring the philosophic mind we try to take our pains with a smiling mouth. A type of spinster exists which affects funerals as the chief of worldly joys. This pleasure in the lugubrious is certainly a trait to be found at least sporadically in the world. Perhaps it existed in the past more frequently than it does now—I hope so. Judge Sewall has this entry in his diary: "Spent the morning in the vault rearranging the family coffins. It was a pleasant but awful treat." This zest for the melancholy is quite another thing, of course, from the response to that beautiful, close harmony, which, though it sound like a discord, is yet so suggestive of the perfect harmony (the ideal) as to make us tremble with delight. I only wish to make the point that there is in human nature some response to a less admirable phase of the dark in life and literature, a kind of ghoulish joy in the grave. The mock-romantic cult in fiction, in the time of Horace Walpole and Mrs. Radcliffe, gives another example. Recall that delicious bit of dialogue in Jane Austen's "Northanger Abbey," where she satirizes the tendency:

" 'But, my dearest Catherine, what have you been doing with yourself all this morning? Have you gone on with Udolpho?'

" 'Yes, I have been reading it ever since I woke; and I am got to the black veil.'

" 'Are you, indeed? How delightful! Oh! I would not tell you what is behind the black veil for the world! Are you not wild to know?'

" 'Oh! yes, quite; what can it be? But do not tell me: I would not be told upon any account. I know it must be a skeleton; I am sure it is Laurentina's skeleton. Oh! I am delighted with the book! I should like to spend my whole life in reading it, I assure you; if it had not been to meet you, I would not have come away from it for all the world.'

" 'Dear creature! how much I am obliged to you; and when you have finished Udolpho, we will read the Italian together; and I have made out a list of ten or twelve more of the same kind for you.'

" 'Have you, indeed! How glad I am! What are they all?'

" 'I will read you their names directly; here they are in my pocketbook: "Castle of Wolfenbach," "Clermont," "Mysterious Warnings," "Necromancer of the Black Forest," "Midnight Bell," "Orphan of the Rhine," and "Horrid Mysteries." Those will last us some time.'

" 'Yes; pretty well; but are they all horrid? Are you sure they are all horrid?'

" 'Yes, quite sure; for a particular friend of mine, a Miss Andrews, a sweet girl, one of the sweetest creatures in the world, has read every one of them.' "

Some rather cynical theories of human nature go even further than this. A distinguished French dramatic critic of our day, in a recent work on the ancient and modern drama, takes the position that our interest in tragedy is at bottom simply the survival of the old savage instinct of cruelty, the enjoyment of suffering. He builds up a whole superstructure of theory upon this foundation. I believe myself that he does great wrong to human psychology in this ingenious assumption, which, however, is interesting as offering one explanation of certain familiar tendencies in modern literature. But one hardly needs to say that all this morbid affecting of the sad is clearly to be distinguished from its proper use in books.

But not the pathetic alone, the awful, too, is common in literature—an element that not so much moves us to tenderness as it freezes us with fear or humbles us with a feeling of our own littleness in the face of the sublime. This influence again, when not out of proportion, can be easily accepted; in fact, the term pleasure may be possibly so enlarged in its meaning as to include this idea. Irving, in his "Conquest of Granada," speaks of the "pleasing terror" begotten in him by the sight of a shaggy Adalusian bull encountered among the mountains of his native wilds. The expression puts before us, epigrammatically, a psychological truth. There is a stern, lofty grandeur in the works of creative genius which constitutes their head-mark of merit. Literature would be poor, indeed, without its Michael Angelos and its Beethovens, its Wagners and its Vereschagins. Their works may not soften, but they strengthen our sinews for the fight. And as we go on in life we gradually come to care more for and to get more from, these austere, great performances. A young man or woman at twenty-one might be inclined to refuse to the terrible a place in literature; the same person at forty might be deriving from that source the most precious part of his or her experience.

Man's attitude toward the awe-inspiring has rapidly changed during the last one hundred and fifty years. English literature registers this fact. Up to the middle of the eighteenth century Alpine scenery was viewed in its horrific, repellent aspects; and when, a few years later, the poet Gray described it as fit stimulus for æsthetic appreciation, he struck a new and, as it then seemed, a bizarre note. Yet, less than a hundred years thereafter, we find Ruskin at his finest of music and majesty in hymning the glories of those Swiss mountains. Awe has widened the hitherto arbitrarily narrow notion of beauty, and the Plutonian forces of Nature are made to minister to spiritual ends. Fear—like unto that fear of the Lord which is the beginning of wisdom—is as beneficent as joy herself.

But literature, and modern literature in special, makes room for other aspects of life besides the appealingly pathetic and the awe-inspiring. The ugly, and the brutal, and the foul are there in crowded cohorts and sickening display. The night side of Nature and the devil side of human nature, these are portrayed at full length. In the literature of the past twenty-five years fiction has a bad preëminence in this respect, though it may be said that the drama has not been very far behind. One's attitude toward the unlovely is naturally of much consequence to oneself and one's fellow men. Has the handling of the degenerate and abnormal— manifestations of which are indubitably to be found in this third planet from the sun—any justification? Is Zola's "Nana" or Daudet's "Sappho" a type instructive enough to make her acquaintance worth while? Is Hardy's "Jude the Obscure," not to say the obscene, a man who can teach us by his wretched failures some life-lesson of value? At a time when some of the very greatest writers alive find a natural expression of their power in such scenes and characters as are suggested by these names, it is imperative for the world of thoughtful, educated readers to take a stand and have an intelligent opinion upon this burning question, condemning with a sweet reasonableness or approving with a like show of sense. We cannot dodge the duty, for the last decade has intensified the danger and made the problem more intricate.

Now, let me say with candor that I think even here we must not be too sweeping, and cry, "Let the ugly be anathema; it is an evil blot on the fair fame of literature." This sort of remark is always popular with the gallery, but it is a careless generalization. Beyond peradventure the ugly— I mean the morally as well as materially ugly—

has a use in literature. There are two ways of
presenting ethical ideals, of making a spiritual
impression: one by showing types of virtue, the
other by showing types of vice. In the former,
we are made to love the good by direct example;
in the latter, to hate the bad, and hence to desire
the good. The methods are respectively positive
and negative; the aim is the same, or may be.

I recall no great English writer who better illustrates the union of these two methods than Robert
Browning. Nobody in his senses disputes the
splendid ethical sanity of this robust seer-singer.
Yet in poem after poem he paints the ravages of
sin in the persons of men and women who possess
a kind of shuddering fascination for the sensitive
admirer of Browning—"Subtlest assertor of the
soul in song." Think of the "Soliloquy of the
Spanish Cloister," with its hideous old monk, his
heart full of envy and hate; of such other churchly
figures as the Bishop who orders his tomb; of
Porphyria's lover, strangling his sweetheart with
her golden hair; of that other woman with golden
hair, the maiden of Pornic, with her horrible greed
for money even in the grave; of many another
light creature with the skin-deep beauty that lures
men on to hell; of the frank fleshliness of the
loves of Ottima and Sebald in "Pippa Passes";
of the loathsome landscape Childe Roland was
forced to look upon; of the searching cynicism of
a brief lyric like "Adam, Lilith and Eve"; and of
the frank approval of active sin, rather than the

half-hearted willing of sin, in "The Statue and the Bust."

Think of these and plenty of other Browning poems, and realize that this man insisted on the dramatic representation of all that is human, whether of good or ill. And yet, who does more to brace us for the spiritual battle-field? No, the test must go deeper than the matter of material or theme; it is the character of the literary creator—his aim and ideal—that settles the thing. Given the right kind of worker behind the work, and no subject, however repulsive, is inadmissible to art—at least in the moral view. Æsthetic considerations there may be which put up the bars against this or that; but the moral result lies in the intention.

When, as not seldom happens, a namby-pamby conventionality sets up to be sole arbiter of such questions, it must be promptly rebuked. I have had this truth impressed upon me in reading of late the newest product of two living writers of international standing,—Tolstoy's novel "Resurrection," and Ibsen's play, "When We Dead Awaken." In the Russian story the protagonists are a harlot on trial for murder and her aristocratic betrayer. One is asked to spend a large part of the time in the government prisons amidst the offscouring of the earth. The realism is insistent, suppressing nothing, telling everything. In this respect the book is most inartistic; it neglects selection, a cardinal virtue in all art.

I may add, in passing, that Tolstoy's technique
has always lacked in this respect; his fellow-coun-
tryman, Turgueneff, was his superior here. But
"Resurrection," in spite of all this, seizes upon
me—what can we do but make confession of our
personal experiences in such a case?—as one of
the noblest and most beautiful works ever put
forth; hardly a masterpiece, because of its defects,
but a deeply moving presentment of man's tragi-
comedy of the years; a wonderful study of a soul
that returns to the good, that "comes to itself,"
in the matchless words of the Bible; and a potent
and eloquent plea for fair dealing between men
and women and for loving kindness even to crim-
inals. Tolstoy is a man with the daring *naïveté*
to try to imitate Christ in his daily life; and both
his life and his work exhale an aroma of righteousness. All his malodorous realism cannot taint those
airs that blow from God. His purpose shines
through it like a light through a sunless cavern.

In Ibsen's drama—a strange, maddeningly mystic deliverance it is, like most of his work for the ten
years past—the conventions are played with fast
and loose, as usual, and to some the piece will do
little but preach the setting aside of marriage
vows in the case of elective affinities. Indeed, one
might almost say of this play that it is Goethe
come again, with an austere mountain setting and
a stern suppression of sentimental gush. And yet,
as I sat rather dazed for some ten minutes after
closing the volume, and let the message have its

way with me—one of those fractions of time which
really count in one's intellectual life—I felt that
there was at least one lesson there for one reader.
The sculptor who used his beautiful model as a
model and never loved her as a woman, though
she had given him her soul, had never truly lived.
They have both made loveless marriages since; but
when they come together again after long years they
are as the dead, and only awaken when they realize
what has been lost. In brief, it is an idealist's
statement of love, a mystic sublimation thereof.
The play is scarcely healthy, but it possesses a
tremendous suggestion touching the world's master-passion.

Caution, then, is the watchword in judging a
great man's handling of the seamy side of life in
literature. This applies to many a so-called purpose novel and problem play of our time, in which
a daring theme is boldly set forth and a degree
of frankness is reached disagreeable to those who
would have their literary path "roses, roses all
the way." Such swinging of the axe may clear
the social trail for a more enlightened civilization.
Fiction like "The Manxman," drama like "The
Second Mrs. Tanqueray," have a place, I dare
avouch, within the broad demesne of art. There
is danger of becoming lax of fibre and limited in
thought-range when they are forbidden. In the
broadest sense, the pleasure got from literature is
in an exhibition of life—an inclusive definition of
literature being that it is a representation of life

in terms of power and beauty. "Memory," says
Balzac in a letter to Madame Hanska, "only registers thoroughly that which is pain. In this sense
it recalls great joy, for pleasure comes very near
to being pain"—a remark in which the modern
psychologist will heartily agree with the French
master. The languid, lackadaisical appreciation
of the sweetly pretty in art is, therefore, a pitiable
impoverishment of the possibilities of literature.
Much of the so-called realistic writing of to-day—
not all of it—can be welcomed as having a genuine mission for men, if only we will extend our
conception of its function.

The dark, we have plead, may be a foil to the
light, which seems to be God's own use of it; it
may spur us on to better things by a graphic picture of things less excellent. Even if it leave us
hopelessly sad—as in the quiet, sardonic pessimism of a fatalist like Hardy, or in a soured re-
former like Ibsen, wrapping himself round in the
protective robes of a baffling mysticism—it may
still be of service in enlarging the sense of life's
ultimate meaning. It can make us weep tears that
have a sweet issue in altruistic endeavor, or awe
us so that never again we break into the "laugh
mistimed in tragic presences."

In the last analysis, perhaps, the only insufferable use of the dark is that which fouls, poisons,
panders to the base; and often this is not somber
at all, but rather speciously glittering and seduc-
tive, like the gaiety of the "Contes Drolatique," the

alluring voluptuousness of "Mademoiselle de Maupin." In current literature we have, God knows, enough of this and to spare. But let us not be hasty to condemn that which in its earnest under purpose and grim largeness belongs to quite another category. As in life, so in literature, aim and ideal are everything. If they be sane and high, it follows, as the night the day, that the author "cannot then be false to any man."

I would thus defend a generous use of the dark in literature. We must be athletic enough to enjoy it, and thoughtful enough to learn its lessons, no more flinching them than we do the lessons of life itself. For literature is not merely an escape from life, though in some of its idyllic moments it may do us minor service of this kind. It is also a criticism of life, in Arnold's phrase, or better, an interpretation of our days and deeds, so that symbol explains fact, and we see not through a glass darkly, but, for the nonce, face to face. And, with a proper placing of the shadows in the background, how lovely is the sunlight, the bird-song, the breath of the cheerful open!

Moral health demands both sides. Burroughs gives good advice when he tells the dyspeptic inclined, to get a taste of something bitter in the woods. A stalwart idealism—which is the only sort wanted — must recognize the divine in and through the dark; else is our light not light, but darkness visible. He who with Merlin follows the gleam shall not win to the Delectable Mountain, save by many a Via Dolorosa, crowded thick with sorry men and women, through the Bad Lands of doubt, agony, sin, and seeming death. It is the price paid for coming at the heights; neither life nor literature can yield their rich rewards by any other bargain.

POETRY AND THE DRAMA

In these days, when there is a marked movement toward bringing poetry and the drama together for the purpose of reëstablishing a literature of the stage, it may not be amiss to say a word concerning their true relations. During the last twenty years, under the influence of Ibsen and his followers, plays have been written and acted in many tongues which made a double appeal; the appeal of drama, something to be heard in the theatre; and the appeal of poetry, a book to be read at home like other books. The divorce of literature and the theatre had been all but universal; France alone, since the time of Moliere, having been true to older ideals of dramatic art. In English-speaking lands the separation has been so complete that many who forget the bygone glories of the Elizabethan stage smile at the idea of any such rehabilitation as is now slowly occurring. Scholars of the cut-and-dried type are slow to wake up to the clear change for the better. Thus, a recent volume with the stimulating title, "Later English Drama," arousing the hope that here is to be discussion of writers such as Pinero, Jones and Shaw, stops short with Bulwer Lytton's "Richelieu" and a single line of contemptuous reference to "such authors as T. W. Robertson, Tom Taylor, Dion Boucicault and W. S. Gilbert"—as if the rest was silence.

But plays are at present being produced by Englishmen, if not by Americans, which are for reading as well as acting. The dramas of Jones, Pinero and Grundy are steadily printed; writers like Comyns Carr, Laurence Irving, W. B. Yeats, Mrs. Craigie and Stephen Phillips produce poetic plays which really get behind the footlights; while novels innumerable are turned into drama-form, and when their maker is a man of the standing of Hardy, Du Maurier or Barrie, help to spread the notion of a literary drama. Even the present remarkable vogue of dramatized novels, which is sneered at in some quarters as a sign of the uncreative condition of the current drama, has at least this use; it serves to suggest to a careless public a possible and profitable relation between books and the stage, the practicableness of bringing together fiction and the play. It might be added that those who regard this reshaping of stories into plays with suspicion, overlook the fact that collaboration was the rule rather than the exception in Shakspere's day, and that the most of his dramas are worked-over stories.

All this is interesting and encouraging. There is reason to think that, more and more, we shall see literature pushing its way into the playhouse; and that, conversely, our poetry will take on dramatic form. So far back as in the eighties Mr. Stedman made a prophecy to that effect in closing

his study of the American poets; and what has
happened since justifies him in a measure. I can
see plainly a desire, which is in several instances
translated into attempts on the part of the younger
verse writers in the United States, to make plays
of poetic quality and yet of dramatic value. The
tentative work of the late Richard Hovey is one
illustration; a recent effort of Mr. William
Vaughn Moody offers another. These, to be sure,
are open to the reproach of being unactable; but
time will teach technique, and the promise is here.

But one thing in regard to the dramatic uses of
poetry must be clearly understood and is most
often overlooked; namely, the drama can and does
exist independently of any of the embellishments
of literature. The latter is an ornament, not a
necessity. By this I mean that a play can be written which is skillful in construction, powerful in
situations, brilliant in characterization, without
having a line in it which deserves to live for its
form's sake. Nay, we may go further and say
that an effective play can be constructed with
no dialogue at all—witness the much-enjoyed
French pantomime which appeared in this country
a few years since. Every practical dramatist is
aware of what a comparatively small function
words have in the upbuilding of a play, where several pages will be given up to an indication of the
"business" and to stage directions, while only a
single sentence perhaps is spoken by the characters. It is well to bear down on this point, be-

cause conventional critics treating the earlier
periods of the literary drama talk as if a play, to
be good, must make enjoyable closet reading.
Nothing is further from the truth.

It is very instructive to study with this thought
in mind the Edwin Booth prompt-books of the
Shakspere plays enacted by that representative
American tragedian. Booth's attitude toward the
poet-dramatist was, as is well-known, entirely reverential; he was a devout student of the dramas
of the master-genius of our race in literature. He
would have been the last to countenance the arbitrary garbling and disfigurement of the plays,
which was not uncommon at the hands of authors
and actors up to Garrick's time. Yet he did not
hesitate to excide ruthlessly passage after passage,
though of the greatest literary value, if they
seemed to him non-dramatic—ornamental, not
vital to the action. A couple of examples will
make this plain.

In "The Merchant of Venice," Bassanio, in his
glowing description of Portia, has this golden
close:

> —"And her sunny locks
> Hang on her temples like a golden fleece;
> Which makes her seat of Belmont Colchos' strand,
> And many Jasons come in quest of her."

No lover of literature would spare these lines;
yet Booth cut them out. Again, in "Hamlet" I,
the Queen in her narration of Ophelia's piteous

death—the whole speech being at the top of the poetry of pathos—ends in this way:

> "Her clothes spread wide;
> And, mermaid-like, awhile they bore her up;
> Which time she chanted snatches of old tunes;
> As one incapable of her own distress
> Or like a creature native and indued
> Unto that element; but long it could not be
> Till that her garments, heavy with their drink,
> Pulled the poor wretch from her melodious lay
> To muddy death."

Here Booth omits what was doubtless to him a most lovely bit of description, but one that too long delayed the action at the very conclusion of the act. There is, of course, nothing in this peculiar to Booth; the whole history of the adaptation of Shakspere's plays to modern conditions of the stage illustrates this tendency to sacrifice poetical adornment for strict dramatic effect. Great moments are to be found in Shakspere, as in all dramatic literature of the loftiest kind, where matchless poetry and intensest drama of the psychologic order unite in a chemical union; these passages and scenes mark the culmination of dramatic literature. But subservient to the purposes of dramatic action, poetry, this fair handmaid of the sterner business of drama, must ever be. It is a cheap begging of the question to say that the reason Shakspere's poetry is suppressed and only his drama in the narrower sense retained is because poetry has now fallen on evil days, whereas in the spacious times of Elizabeth that highest expression of the imagination met a sympathetic response. Rather should it be said that we now have a clearer conception of the proper limits of play-making and realize as never before that to block action even by putting beauty in its way is bad technique in the drama. It may be remarked also that the practical reshaping of many Shakspere plays for the purposes of modern representation is a further example of the firmer dramatic construction of our day,—not necessarily an iconoclastic outrage at all. It is true that in the stage history of Shakspere we find that unwarranted liberties have been taken with his text, with his characters, even with the fundamental idea of his dramas, so that a play like "King Lear" is emasculated by a "happy ending." The period of the Restoration was a chief sinner in this respect; so late as the eighteenth century an actor-manager like Garrick takes undue liberties. But the adaptations familiar in our own time are quite another matter. The habit is justified by the results. The late Mr. Daly's occasional revivals, where the dramas were presented intact, and which were lauded to the skies for their reverential spirit toward the original text, in pleasing contrast with the profane handling thereof more often seen, only served to strengthen the argument in favor of needed changes. Mr. Mansfield's rendition of "Henry V" offers a case in point at the present writing. One who witnessed his performance with the regular text in hand was hard put to it to fol-

low the lines, so freely were scenes pulled about
and passages excided. Yet it were foolish to deny
the gain in compression and coherence, this rebuild-
ing being particularly legitimate in the case of
one of the history-chronicle plays, which from
their very nature are more loosely constructed
than a drama like "Hamlet" or "Lear" or "Mac-
beth," where a deep psychologic significance draws
the parts together in a more than molecular marriage. The reader will find a further treatment
of this improvement in dramatic technique in the
following essay.

This fact of the separate aim of literature and
the drama is no argument against their union.
Though independent, they make the strongest of
allies. But it does suggest a caution against
sneering at the so-called unliterary drama, which,
if well done in accordance with the laws of stage-
craft, is admirable and fulfills its immediate purpose. Ah, yes, its immediate purpose; therein lies
the criticism. If the playwright would do more
than succeed at once; if he would be treasured in
after days, let him do as did Shakspere and his
fellows, Congreve and the Restoration men, Sheridan and Goldsmith in the last century; and as
Ibsen, Maeterlinck, Hauptmann, Sudermann,
Rostand and Stephen Phillips are doing in our
own time; let him, in addition to human interest
and technical structure, bedeck the play in the fair
garments of poetry, bejewel it, as it were, with the
ideal, and present the more impassioned moments

of character in language that is fittingly poetic because at such times life itself becomes lyrical, heroic, dramatic in a noble sense. For it must be remembered that poetry is, after all, more than ornament; it is stuff of the very essence of a moment when life is at its keenest and highest and broadest. There is a poetry of situation on the stage irrespective of language; and when the words used are proper to the scene they are far more than decoration, being rather the permanent registration through the expressional medium of speech of what were otherwise a fleeting sight— part of a play that has its run and then ceases to be—perhaps forever. The strongest plea for the union of poetry and the stage is, then, that the poetry that is in action in the interrelations of human beings must be fine-languaged to get itself all-expressed and long-preserved. Then shall the play-makers be praised within the theatre and also be read with delight; and shall be names for children's children to conjure with. The signs are not few that this laudable marriage of play and poetry is taking place once more in our time, late illustrations being furnished by Stephen Phillips' striking dramatic rehabilitation of the old but immortally beautiful Francesca da Rimini story and his boldly fine handling of a biblical motive in "Herod."

THE DEVELOPMENT OF TECHNIQUE IN THE DRAMA

The truth that the drama is a form of literature having its own technique seems obvious enough. Yet if one may judge by many attempts at play-making and much literary criticism, it is a fact so occult as to have escaped general observation. It is only of late, with the great demand for the turning of alleged dramatic fiction into play form, that novelists as a class have come to accept the idea that the art of fiction is one, that of the stage another. Too often in the past has it been assumed that because a piece of fiction is what we call "dramatic," it will surely make a strong play; that a situation in a novel can be transplanted bodily for use upon the boards. Every year still the failures of dramatised fiction are to be explained by this assumption. There is in the growing practice of calling on collaborating dramatists of practical experience for help, a significant admission by authors that the lack of such knowledge is likely to be fatal. The difference in the respective methods of fiction and the drama is, as a matter of fact, almost as great as that between essay and poetry.

The indiscriminating praise of Shakspere, master poet of the race, reveals the same tendency to overlook this fundamental distinction. It has become the most threadbare of commonplace to allow to him all the claims possible to be filed by a maker of literature. It is a matter of course to deal only in superlatives when discoursing on the Stratford man. Hence has grown up a habit, careless with those who know better, and ignorant and mistaken in the case of critics who do not think for themselves,—the habit of confusing the technique of the Elizabethan dramatists, inclusive of Shakspere, with the splendid poetry which adorned that stage and makes it unique in English literature.

Shakspere was confronted with the tremendous task of establishing the art of play-writing in England; in view of what he found when he began, he performed a miracle in leaving dramatic technique what it was when he had rounded out his mighty play-cycle with the romances, "Cymbeline," "The Winter's Tale," and "The Tempest." To appreciate this, however, it is necessary to read and digest the precedent attempts at play literature: the crude, coarse comedies of "Ralph Roister Doister" and "Gammer Gurton's Needle;" the frigid lifelessness of "Gorbudoc," with its slavish imitation of the Senecan models; the vital but often childishly ineffective and shapeless tragedies of Marlowe;—to say nothing of the tentative efforts of men like Peele, Greene, Kyd and Nash. In comparison, Shakspere's plays seem to leap Cadmus-like at the creative word into full strength.

But this is all relative. Looking back, one sees that the poet-player founded modern dramatic method and clothed it on with a splendor unsurpassed; but looking forward towards our own time, and thinking of play-making as such, he is to be recognized as a very great journeyman learning to use his tools, gradually sloughing off excrescences inevitable to the artistic beginnings of any literary craft; in few, he exhibits a progressive mastery of technique marvellous for his day but falling short in many ways of the perfection of dramatic art which was to be reached in the evolution of over three hundred years. In the creation of character, in the poetic interpretation of human life, Shakspere stands alone; but in the manipulation of the play-form for the purposes of dramatic exposition, he has been left far behind. The technique of an Ibsen, a Hauptmann, a Pinero, a Gillette, is far superior, if by technique be meant the adaptation of means to a certain end. This sort of remark is commonly heard when intelligent students come together for talk, and yet are they cautious of saying it in print. Yet surely it is no detraction from Shakspere's genius to make the point. To deny it is to call Shakspere not a man but a god, and (which is worse) to set aside one of the cardinal principles of all fruitful literary criticism; namely, that literature is a growth, and that even genius has its relation to environment, its limitations of time and place.

A certain class of minds takes particular satisfaction in pooh-poohing art and emphasizing personality. Shakspere, it holds, could create dramatic technique about as easily as he could write peerless blank verse. One who adopts this as a working hypothesis in the study of literature—or of any art—will get in a sad muddle. Its violation of the idea of literature as an organic growth, not a fortuitous combination of human atoms, makes it untenable in a day when the evolutionary principle is so firmly founded.

But how, it may be asked, have plays gained so wonderfully as to make the best modern drama more admirable than that of the early giants? What are the improvements which mark technique to-day and often make a play an example of fine art? A study of English stage literature from the late sixteenth century to the present furnishes the answer. I shall try to point out a few of the significant changes, the substantial gains.

To bring many particulars under a common denominator, it may be said that the improvement in dramatic method since the Elizabethans has all been in the direction of greater truth in the portrayal of life; almost all the changes have been in the interests of vraisemblance. Little by little, outworn devices, antiquated conventions, originally useful but eventually lacking life, clumsy attempts to depict what was not demanded by the dramatic necessity, and features which were in reality only admitted because of a confusion of dramatic form with such other forms as romance or epic were all dropped under a clearer apprehension of the essential purpose of drama,—the telling of a story by characters in action and within definitely circumscribed material bounds.

Shakspere himself was a pioneer in this reform; he ridded the stage of many of the imperfections which were clogging the development of English drama. He greatly reduced the rôle of the rhyming couplet in tragedy, thereby freeing the spirit of poetry from a narrow and unnatural convention. He breathed the breath of life under the stark ribs of blank verse by breaking up the full line into the irregular dialogue which imitated the very quiver of human nature. A glance at the pre-Shaksperean tragedy with its absurdly unnatural regularity of verse movement will make this plain. He excised the rambling episodic matter which made those earlier plays a lumber room of loose unrelated material. He went far towards eliminating the chorus, the masque, and dumbshow features that, however attractive in themselves, were as millstones checking the free play of drama. He broke up the acts of the play into scenes, thereby showing a sense of the drama as tableau, something consisting of successive stage pictures that must compose even as a picture "composes." He destroyed the tyranny of the classic writers which up to his coming fairly choked dramatic action and motive. By introducing comedy into drama whose ground plan was tragic, he produced an effect of reality never before secured,—a change iconoclastic to a degree now difficult to appreciate. He began to denote "business" and to insert stage directions, his work in this respect being but tentative, a step in the right path. Students having in hand one of the many modern editions of Shakspere with their full equipment in the way of change of scene, stage direction, and business, and all that goes to the explication of the text, would do well to look at a fac-simile reproduction of the First Folio of 1623 in order to realize how much has been added by the editorial supervision of well-nigh three centuries. But the main fact is, that Shakspere's contributions to the advancement, indeed the founding of dramatic technique, have been many and remarkable.

Nevertheless, the English drama as he left it and as it was handled by the late and post-Elizabethans was full of defects and even absurdities. It was loosely constructed, for one important thing. There was a lack of unity which strikes the present-day student with astonishment when he examines even a masterpiece by Shakspere and finds that it is easy to shift the order of the scenes to the improvement of the action, a closer-knit and more sequential effect being produced. The loose arrangement of the scenes in an Elizabethan play can be explained in two ways; in the first place, in many dramas, especially the chronicle history plays of which "Richard III" and "Henry V" are excellent illustrations, the principal aim was to offer a series of more or less loosely related spectacles, each effective in itself; the author cared less about an organic story. The second and chief reason lies in the physical conditions of the stage of that time, the very lack of scenery making scenes possible. For when such a scenic change does not call for new scenery, there is no managerial objection to it; whereas, if every change means a considerable financial outlay, the ambitious playwright will find himself at loggerheads with the practical man of the theatre. It is in such material facts that the multiplicity of scenes in many Elizabethan dramas—as high as ten or a dozen to an act in some instances—has its origin, a crude sense of art also helping to bring about such a result. Pass from such plays to a late modern example, and you will find an Ibsen rarely allowing more than two scenes to an act; while Bernard Shaw, who is an extremist in the simplification and perfecting of stage technique, regularly makes the scene co-extensive with the act.

The later Elizabethan drama was also notable for its monstrosities of plot. Shakspere, though avoiding the worst of them, did not hesitate to make use of the conventions which sacrificed the sense of realities, as in his treatment of sex disguises so common from the time of an early piece like "Two Gentlemen of Verona." In a genuinely strong play like "The Merchant of Venice" the verisimilitude is greatly injured by the assumption that Portia in her charming lawyer's robes really hides her identity; as a matter of fact, her personality is no more cloaked than is that of a girl college student who as Commencement draws near dons her Oxford gown and so lends a piquant touch to the June campus. This example may serve to stand for numerous concessions on Shakspere's part to stage traditions antagonistic to the truthful interpretation of life in the theater. It should be remembered, too, that the custom of boy actors for the woman parts introduced further complications and concessions. Shakspere's worst lapse in this matter or in other departures from truth were as nothing compared with such a congeries of wild and fantastic horrors as is to be met with in Webster's "Duchess of Malfi,"—a play, which contains, notwithstanding, poetry as magnificent as can be found in the whole range of Elizabethan drama. The tendency of the post-Elizabethans in this matter of realism of incident and character and the skillful adjustment of action to end, was swiftly downhill.

But with the drama of the Restoration came an improvement. There was a loss of poetry, of the imaginative appeal to the abiding interests and passions. But in technique, and given their object, the plays of Congreve and his mates certainly show an advance,—a dialogue notably better in lifelikeness and a far abler handling of the story, which often is so clearly articulated that effect flows from cause without hitch or violation

of truth. To explain the brilliant reflection of
social manners seen in the best known dramas of
Goldsmith and Sheridan, one must read the earlier
plays of Congreve, Farquhar, Van Brugh and
Wycherly. By the time the Restoration period is
reached, we have dispensed with much extraneous
matter common with the Elizabethans: the inter-
polated dumb show, the purely undramatic masque,
the common use of long descriptive passages
which, however beautiful, clogged action and the
display of character; the clumsy introduction of
the supernatural, as in the closing act of "Cymbeline." Obviously, a part of this change is due to
the very different nature of the later drama, which
is a comedy of manners where before was romantic
tragedy. We have left the world which labors
and loves in the noble sense for the little corrupt
world of town intrigue and pleasure. But beyond
doubt a main reason is the increased sense of what
the dramatic requirements are. Dryden's criticism
of the stage and stage literature gives valuable testimony to this keener appreciation in his day of
the methods of play-writing that is intended for
stage representation.

Furthermore, it were absurd to suppose that
with the eighteenth century—including such delightful and familiar productions as "She Stoops
to Conquer" and "The School for Scandal"—the
last word in the evolution of dramatic method was
spoken. The aim in those dramas was the exposition of social types and customs,—a satiric inten-

tion; hence brilliant dialogue and clearcut portraiture within definitely prescribed limits. But the story invented to carry these characteristics is, compared with the ingenious inventions of later playwrights and the vital imaginings of a few, thin, slight and not seldom unconvincing enough. An impression of talk at the expense of action is conveyed, overcome partially, at least, in our day by casting the piece with such capable actors that their superb art makes us forget defects of composition. Yet the Bancrofts in London, confronted by these facts, did not hesitate to edit "The School for Scandal." In witnessing the famous screen scene in that drama, it is impossible not to feel the conventionality and flimsiness of the situation, if one will but fix the mind on the play rather than upon the acting itself. All this comes out clearly in a performance of the play by amateurs; there is little in the piece to carry it of itself. It needs resourceful players; whereas, Pinero's "Sweet Lavender," or Grundy's "A Pair of Spectacles" are comedies which give pleasure if enacted by high school students. Indifferent or bad acting cannot kill them.

The complete disappearance of the chorus, another classic tradition often used by Shakspere, is a mark of modern work that has its significance. It means that for strict dramatic purposes, comment, no matter if it be the beautiful lyric comment of the Attic drama, is an excrescence. The theory of dramatic art which admits of choragic

interpolation is entirely contrary to present-day
ideas. If the aim be poetic justice in the interpretation of life, this custom may still be defended;
the Japanese use it now in their drama. But with
the stern insistence on action as the kernel of
drama, it had to go, to the palpable advantage of
dramatic effect. But the crowds in the background
of melodramas and historical tragedies and sometimes of romantic comedies, clusters of people who
shout in unison or become vocal through a spokesman, are plainly a survival of the Greek chorus.
It is instructive, therefore, to notice how they are
got rid of in the best constructed current drama.
Of course in historical plays and all dramas of
strong scenic possibilities the supernumerary is
more likely to appear and has a sort of justification as picturesque accessory. But on the whole
the most masterly drama of to-day handles this
attenuated chorus gingerly if at all. Its free use
even in the spectacular play-work of a Sardou now
makes an impression of old-fashionedness.

The cutting out of episodic material is an important element in this bettering of technique.
The so-called induction of the Elizabethans is ill
tolerated at present; only as the prologue in plays
sensationally incident-full. The Christopher Sly
episode in Shakspere's "Taming of the Shrew"
is a case in point. In most modern representa-
tions it is omitted; in that, for example, made
familiar to Americans by the Daly company. In
the staging of the piece by Miss Ada Rehan this

induction was restored, no doubt to the amusement of the audiences which enjoyed the unctuous humor of the scene, but just as truly to the detriment of the main action; for the purpose of a first act,—to begin the story,—is obscured when the mind is thus started on a wrong scent, however attractive the game. A sense of irritation is produced on the realization that here is a play within a play without Hamlet's excuse. Spencer's law of the economy of attention would explain the wrong to dramatic construction here done.

The general adjustment of costume to impersonation during the development of the drama was but an outward and visible sign of that general approximation to life itself on the stage already explained. With the Elizabethans, verisimilitude of dress, like verisimilitude of scenery, was little sought. Money was spent freely at times, especially on court masques and revels. More money was paid for a velvet cloak than for the copyright of a play. But the sense of historical accuracy or the desire to copy social externals hardly existed. Wild absurdities of costume are to be noted in all stages of the English drama from the morality plays to the modern period; so late as the eighteenth century the dresses of the ladies in a classical play were wholly of the age of powder and patches. There was likewise small demand at first for that truth of dialogue which means that each person of the play shall properly pronounce words suitable to his or her station, dialectic variations from normal English being given with exquisite exactitude and great skill by the players. The rendering of the rustic speech of New England in a play like Herne's "Shore Acres," of that of the South in Mr. Thomas's "Alabama" or of provincial England in "Tess" is so far superior to the clumsy phonetics of the early drama as to take on the importance of a new art. Compare with the best examples of this care in the reproduction of speech on the stage, the attempt in Shakspere's "Henry V" to give the dialects of the Welsh, Irish and Scotch soldiers, and a realization of the difference, the immense progress, will be gained.

Truth of scene has gone hand in hand with truer costume and speech in the modern play. The illusion wrought by placing the *dramatis personae* in a congruous environment, is a very great aid in impressing the auditor with a sense of life. The objections so often urged against the elaborateness of modern scenery are all aimed at the abuse of a good thing,—the overwhelming of action by ornament. To argue, as some critics do, that there might have been more appeal to the imagination—and hence as a result more appreciation of dramatic poetry,—in the bare accessories of the Elizabethan stage, seems to be a scholar's fad rather than a reasonable objection to such stage-setting as shall make for illusion. The consideration of a play as, among other things, a pictorial appeal, has its psychological side. In a recent paper, Mr. Thomas, a well known native playwright, dilated upon the modern dramatist's recognition of the necessity of carefully studied color schemes in the successive scenes of a play, relative to the nature of the drama itself: making the point that a play might be made or marred according as the dramatist kept this requirement in mind. Many such a finesse is given due weight in latter day dramatic technique.

One of the most persistent of stage conventions is the "aside;" its effect is always to destroy illusion, and in plays of our day whenever it is used the auditor simply concedes to the playwright a departure from realism for the sake of convenience. To speak lines nominally *sotto voce* in such tones as shall be heard from every seat of a large theater and are yet *ex hypothesi* not overheard by sundry persons on the stage, is an absurdity only tolerated for its supposed helpfulness in explaining the situation or explicating the plot. In the best modern dramas the "aside" is coming to be used more and more charily; by Ibsen, for instance, in his social satires. In an occasional play —this is true of William Gillette's "Held By The Enemy," "Secret Service," and "Sherlock Holmes" —this time-honored device is entirely dispensed with. The additional demand on the author's ingenuity is apparent, but the gain in truthfulness and so in strength of impression, well repays the effort. It is safe to say that modern technique will fast eliminate the "aside."

Much the same evolution may be traced in the matter of the soliloquy. But here a complete abandonment of a stage trick which is inimical to lifelikeness, is harder and slower, for there is a certain psychologic justification for it, not found at all in the case of the "aside." People think out their situations when alone, and to give those thoughts vocal utterance is a pardonable objectifying of a common subjective experience. Moreover, people actually do soliloquize when under mental or emotional strain; many of us know this from our own habit. Still, clever playwrights to-day are reducing the rôle of the soliloquy in a marked way, and now and then its total disappearance in a play is to be chronicled. Here again Mr. Gillette is in the van, his dramas already mentioned being constructed without a concession to a convention which in Shakspere is inwrought with the very texture of the dramaturgic effect.

The reduction in the number of the persons of the play and the simplification of the act divisions are still other tendencies of modern technique. Glance at a typical Ibsen drama and see how prevailingly the piece is cast for six or eight parts. In "Ghosts" the number is but five; which is also true of English playwrights like Pinero. Compare this restriction with the Elizabethan habit. The contrast is startling. The exceptions to this rule are found in historical dramas like Rostand's "L'Aiglon" with its fifty and more persons; or

Sardou's "Robespierre," with hardly a less number. In these there is really a reversal to older methods,—a tendency in the last named plays extending to the use of six acts. The evolution in the habit of division into acts has been steadily towards a reduction of the number. With the Greeks the play fell into episodes rather than into acts in the modern sense. Nowadays, while the old distribution into five acts allowing for the introduction, growth, height, fall and catastrophe is still found in heavy tragedy, comedy has shrunk to a customary three acts, and tragedy that deals with contemporary persons and scenes either to three or four, with a preference in romantic plays with heavily dramatic situations for four. Nor is this change arbitrary. It indicates a feeling for simplification which recognizes the tripartite life in a properly built play, it being a creature having a beginning, middle, and end, the additional act being in reality a subdivision of the second act. Since this scheme of construction is fundamental, it seems likely that technique will come to settle on three acts as the normal arrangement, a departure therefrom being due to special needs or restrictions—as in the case of the historical play which, like the historical novel, has a method all its own.

Even from this rapid *coup d'œil* at the development of dramatic technique it can be understood that we have here a healthy growth which has now reached a high degree of perfected art. To turn the back on present-day play-making as if it had no interest, the dramatic glories of the past being alone worth while, is a foolish phase of conservatism. It arises in part from the confusion of two separate things, drama and literature, which, however happy in their marriage, are independent organisms. It is one of the encouraging signs of current drama that along with an immense improvement in technique, is now to be noted such cultivation of the literary aspects of the play, as is giving the stage dramas enjoyable not only in actual presentation but for private reading. If we may never again expect the creative genius of a Shakspere, surely we have some compensation in the truthful portrayal of human life on the stage and in the abler manipulation of stage artifice to bring about that very desirable result.

THE ESSAY AS MOOD AND FORM

It is odd that while the essay as a distinctive form in modern literature is so well cherished and enjoyable, it has received so little of expert attention. Books upon the drama, upon poetry in its many phases, upon the novel even—a thing comparatively of but yesterday—are as leaves on Vallombrosa for number; but books on the essay —where are they? It is high time the natural history of the essay was written, for here is a fascinating literary development which has had a vigorous, distinguished life of more than three hundred years in English and which counts among its cultivators some of the abiding names in our native literature. Here is a form, too, interesting because of its inter-filiations with such other forms as fiction which is connected with it by the bridge of the character-sketch; drama, whose dialogue the essay not seldom uses; and such later practical offshoots as the newspaper editorial and the book review.

This neglect of the essay is not altogether inexplicable. Scholars have been shy of it, I fancy, in part at least, because on the side of form (the natural and proper side to consider in studying the historical evolution of a literary genre) it has been thus fluent and expansive: a somewhat subtle, elusive thing. We can say, obviously, that an essay is a prose composition, but can we be more explicit than this rather gross mark of identification? The answer is not so easy. Moreover, the question has become further confused by a change in the use and meaning of the word within a century. A cursory glance at the history of the English essay will make this plain.

Lord Bacon was, by his own statement, fond of that passed master of the essay in French, Montaigne. It is small wonder then that, when at the end of the sixteenth century he put a name to his "dispersed meditations," he called them essays, after the Frenchman, using the word for the first time in our tongue. Not the name only but the thing was new. The form was slight, the expression pregnant and epigrammatic; there was no attempt at completeness. The aim of this early prince of essayists was to be suggestive rather than exhaustive—the latter a term too often synonymous with exhausting. Bacon's essays imply expanded note-book jottings; indeed, he so regarded them. In the matter of style, one has but to read contemporaries like Sidney, Lyly and Hooker, to see to what an extent Lord Bacon modernized the cumbersome, though often cloudily splendid, Elizabethan manner. He clarified and simplified the prevailing diction, using shorter words and crisper sentences with the result of closer knit, more sententious effect. In a word, Style became more idiomatic, and the re-

lation of author and reader more intimate in the
hands of this Elizabethan essay-maker. The point
is full of significance for the history of this alluring form; its development ever since has been
from this initiative. Slight, casual, rambling,
confidential in tone, the manner much, the theme
unimportant in itself, a mood to be vented rather
than a thought to add to the sum of human
knowledge; the frank revelation of a personality
—such have been and are the head marks of the
essay down to the present day. This fact is somewhat obscured by our careless use of the word at
present to denote the formal paper, the treatise:
the current definition of the essay admits this extension, and of course we bandy the word about in
such meaning. But it is well to remember that
the central idea of this form is what removes it
forever from the treatise, from any piece of writing that is formal, impersonal and communicative
of information. Little was done for the development of the essay, after Bacon, during the seventeenth century. But with Addison, Steele and the
Spectator in the early eighteenth, the idea is re-
inforced and some of the essential features of this
form brought the more clearly out. The social,
chatty quality of the true essayist is emphasized;
the writer enters into more confidential relations
with his reader than ever he did with the stately
Verulam; and the style approaches more nearly
to the careless, easy elegance of the talk of good,
but not stiff society. The Spectator papers un-

questionably did more to shape the mold of essay writing in English than any other influence; at the same time, to speak as if Mr. Bickerstaff originated the form (as some critics do), is to overlook its origin with Bacon. The essay idea—this colloquial, dramatic, esoteric, altogether charming sort of screed, was cultivated quite steadily through the eighteenth century. It became, as a rule, more ponderous in the hands of Johnson and was in danger of taking on a didactic, hortatory tone foreign to its nature; yet occasionally in the "Rambler" papers, Johnson takes on a lightness of touch and tone that is surprising and suggests that we have perhaps regarded the dictator as too exclusively a wielder of sesquipedalian words. That this God of the Coffee House had a clear and correct idea of the essay is shown by his own description of it: "A loose sally of the mind," he says, "an irregular, indigested piece, not a regular and orderly performance."

Goldsmith, a light-horse soldier in contrast with Johnson, full panoplied and armed cap-a-pie, broadened the essay for literary and social discussion, although Grub Street necessity led him at times to become encyclopedic; and he was never happier than when, as in "The Revery at the Boar's Head" he played upon some whimsical theme, pizzicato, surcharging it with his genial personality. Minor writers, too, in the late eighteenth century had a hand in the development; none more so, to my mind, than the letter and fiction makers, Chesterfield and Walpole, Lady Mary Wortley Montagu and Fanny Burney—these and that inimitable fuss and chronicler, Boswell. If one would know how society talked in the second half of that Tea Cup century, one must read—not the dialogue of the novelists where the art is too new to have caught quite the accent of life, but these off-hand epistles dashed off without a thought of print—to print were half way vulgar then—and hence possessing all the freshness and naturalness of life itself,—the ideal essay note. We may be thankful that as yet the habit of publishing everything, from one's thrills to one's table tastes, had not gained popularity,—those ladies and gentlemen could afford to be charmingly unreserved in their private correspondence. To-day in the very act of penning a note, intrudes the horrid thought that it may be incorporated as an integral part of one's "works."

The Letter, as a literary form, offers an interesting line of side inquiry in connection with the essay; it has influenced that form beyond doubt, is in a sense contributory to it. In the same way dialogue—a modern instance like Landor comes to mind—has had its share in shaping so protean a form.

But it was reserved for the nineteenth century to contribute in the person of Charles Lamb the most brilliant exemplar of the essay, prince of this special literary mood; not primarily a

thinker, a knowledge-bringer, a critic, but just a
unique personality expressing his ego in his own
fascinating way, making the past pay rich toll,
yet always himself; and finding the essay accom-
modative of his whimsical vagaries, his delicious
inconsistencies, his deep-toned, lovable nature.
And that incomparable manner of his! 'Tis at
once richly complex and tremulously simple; an
instrument of wide range from out whose keys a
soul vibrant to the full meaning of humanity
might call spirits of earth and heaven in exquisite
evocations and cadences at times almost too pierc-
ing sweet. Turn to the Elia papers and see
how perfectly this magic of Lamb's illustrates and
supports the qualities of mood and form I am
naming as typical of the essay as an historic
growth. The themes, how desultory, audacious,
trivial, even grotesque. The only possible justification for a dissertation on roast pig is the paper
itself. Note, too, how brief some of the choicest
essays are; half a dozen small pages, even less;
and with what seeming carelessness they vary,
stretching themselves at will to four times their
normal length. Study the construction of any
famous essay to see if it can be called close-knit,
organic, and you shall find a lovely disregard of
any such intention. The immortal Mrs. Battle
on whist gives a capital example. If you turn to
the end of that inimitable deliverance, you will
find it to contain one of the most charming digressions in all literature. Lamb leaves that deli-

cious old gentlewoman for a moment to speak of Cousin Bridget, Bridget Elia, the tragic sister Mary of his house, and playfully, tenderly, picturing their game at cards, forgets all else and never returns to Mrs. Battle. But who cares? Is not lack of organic connection (to call it by so harsh a name) more than justified by that homely-heartful picture of Charles and Mary Lamb, bent over their "mere shade of play,"—a game not for shillings but for fun—nay, for love. "Bridget and I should be ever playing," says he, and the reader is charmed and stirred clean out of all thought of Mrs. Battle. It is ever so with your essayist to the manner born! to wander and digress is with him a natural right. He is never happier than when he is playing mad pranks with logic, respectability and the mother tongue. Yet should his temperament be sensitive, his nature broad, deep and noble. The querulous-gentle Elia was surely of this race.

To turn from Lamb to any contemporary is an effect of anticlimax. None other was like to him for quality. Yet Hazlitt and Hunt were his helpers, doing good work in extending the gamut of this esoteric mood in literature. DeQuincy, too, though losing the essay touch again and again because of didacticism and a sort of formal, stately eloquence, wrote papers in the true tradition of the essayist. Passages in the "Opium Eater" are of this peculiar tone and that great writer's intense subjectivity is always in his favor—since

the genuine essay-maker must be frankly an
egoist. Hunt is at times so charming, so light of
touch, so atmospheric in quality that he deserves
to be set high among essayists of the early century.
A man who could produce such delicately graceful
vignette work as his sketches of the Old Lady and
the Old Gentleman, was a true commensal of
Lamb. In such bits of writing the mood and
manner are everything, the theme is naught; the
man back of the theme is as important in the production of the essay as is the man back of the
gun in warfare. Herein lies Hunt's chief claim
on our grateful remembrance—here, and in certain of his verses, rather than in the more elab-
orate papers to be found in such a volume as
"Fancy and Imagination."

But already we must begin to recognize in
writers like Hunt, Hazlitt and DeQuincy, and
still more in latter men, a tendency distinctly
modern and on the whole antagonistic to the peculiar virtues of the esoteric essay, the *causerie* of
literature. It is moving fast toward the objective, rounded out, formally arranged treatise. It
becomes argumentative, critical, acquisitive,
logical, expository, laden with thought. Hence
when we reach masters like Ruskin, Carlyle,
Arnold, we see what is natural to them as essayists in one sense deflected into other (and no
doubt quite as welcome) forms; one and all, they
have messages, and missions. Now your bona fide
essayist has nothing of the kind; he would simply

button-hole you for a half hour while he talks garrulously, without a thought of purpose, about the world—and himself—especially the latter. Splendid blooms grow from out the soil which gives us our Ruskins and Carlyles; but when we are considering this sensitive plant of the literary garden, the essay, it were well to agree that it is another thing, and to save for its designation the word essay. Nor is this to deny essay touches, essay moments, essay qualities to Ruskin or Carlyle; it is only to make the point that their strenuous aim and habitual manner, so far as they went, were against the production of a very different kind of literature.

Earlier American literature has at least supplied one real essayist to the general body of English literature,—the genial Irving, who was nurtured on the best eighteenth century models and carried on the tradition of the Spectator and Goldsmith in papers which have just the desired tone of genteel talk, the air of good society. There are hints in Benjamin Franklin that had politics not engulfed him, as they afterward did Lowell, he might have shown himself to the essay born. Irving is sometimes spoken of as a fictionist, but all his stories have the essay mood and manner; and he had the good sense practically never to abandon that gentle genre. His work always possesses the essay touch both in description and in the hitting off of character, thus offering an illustration of the fact that the essay, by way of

the character sketch, debouches upon the broad
and beaten highway of the novel,—the main road
of our modern literature. There are plenty of Irving's papers which it is rather puzzling to name
as essay or fiction; "The Fat Gentleman," for example. A later and very true American essayist,
Dr. Holmes, furnishes the same puzzle in the
Autocrat series: they have dialogue, dramatic
characterization, even some slight story interest.
Why not fiction then? Because the trail of the
genuine essayist is everywhere; the characters, the
dramatic setting, are but devices for the freer expression of Dr. Holmes's own delightful personality, which, as Mr. Howells testifies, Holmes liked
to objectify. It is our intimate relation with him
that we care about in converse with the essayist
born; we sit down to enjoy his views. The fictionist's purpose, contrariwise, is to show life in a
representative section of it and with dramatic in-
terplay of personalities moving to a certain
crescendo of interest called the climax.

And so Dr. Holmes remains one of our most
distinctive and acceptable essayists of the social
sort—possessing, I mean, that gift, perhaps best
seen with the French, of making vivid one's sense
of one's relation to other men and women in the
social organism. It is the triumph of this kind
of essay to be at once individualistic and social;
without eccentricity, on the one hand, or vulgarity,
on the other. Vulgarity, by the way, is a quality
impossible to the heaven-called essayist; it can be

better tolerated in poetry even. For the intimacy between the essayist and his reader (I say reader rather than audience with a feeling that the relation is a sort of solitude *à deux*) is greater than in the case of any other form of literary expression; hence, when one enters, as it were, the inner rooms of a friend's house, any hint of the *borné* is the more quickly detected, the more surely insufferable.

The voice of a natural essayist like Thoreau is somewhat muffled by being forced now and then into the public pulpit manner. Yet an essay-writer by instinct he certainly is; particularly in his journal, but often in the more formal chroniclings of his unique contact with nature. In Emerson, too, we encounter a writer with a vocation for the essay, but having other fish to fry,—doubtless a loftier aim but a different. No man, English or American, has a literary manner which makes the essay an inspired chat more than the Concord sage-singer; and the inspired chat comes close to being the beau ideal of your true-blue essayist. With less strenuousness of purpose and just a bit more of human frailty—or at least sympathy with the frail,—here were indeed a prince in this kind!

How much of the allurement of the essay style did Lowell keep, however scholarlike his quest, in papers literary, historical, even philological! In a veritable essay-subject like "On a Certain Condescension in Foreigners," he displays himself as of the right line of descent from Montaigne; there is in him then all that unforced, winsome, intimate, yet ever restrained revelation of self which is the essayist's model, and despair. In the love letters of the Brownings may be found some strictures by both Robert and Elizabeth upon an early book of this great American's which must pain the admirer of the Brownings as well as of Lowell. It displays a curious insensitiveness to just this power of the Cambridge man which made him of so much more value to the world than if he had been scholar and nothing more. One can hardly rise from anything like a complete examination of Lowell's prose without the regret that his fate did not lead him to cultivate more assiduously and single-eyed, this rare and precious gift for essay—a gift shared with very few fellow Americans.

A glance among later Victorian prose writers must convince the thoughtful that the essay in our special sense is gradually written less; that as information comes in at the door, the happy giving-forth of personality flies out at the window. It is in shy men like Alexander Smith or Richard Jefferies that we come on what we are looking for, in such as they, rather than the more noisily famed. Plenty of charming prosists in these latter days have been deflected by utility or emolument away from the essay; into criticism, like Lang and Gosse and Dobson and Pater; into preaching and play-making, like Bernard Shaw;

into journalism like Barry Pain and Quiller-Couch; into a sort of forced union of poetry and fiction, as with Richard LeGallienne. All of these, too, and others still have been touched by fiction for better or worse.

The younger Americans with potential essay ability are also for the most part swallowed up in more practical, "useful" ways of composition. Her old-fashioned devotion to the elder idea of the essay makes a writer like Miss Repplier stand out with a good deal of distinction, so few of her generation are willing or able to do likewise. There is no magazine in America to-day, with the honorable exception of "The Atlantic," which desires from contributors essays that look back to the finer tradition. Mr. Howells has reached a position of such authority in American letters that what he produces in the essay manner is welcome—not because it is essay, but because it is he. His undeniable gift for the form is therefore all the better; often he strikes a gait happily remindful of what the essay in its traditions really is; the delightfully frank egoism of his manner covering genuine simplicity and modesty of nature. Since "Venetian Days" he has never ceased to be an essayist.

The twin dangers with the younger essayists of both the United States and England are didacticism and preciosity. The former I believe most prevalent in this country; and it is of course the death blow of the true essay. The danger of being too precious may be overcome with years: Max Beerbohm, for example, began by thinking and talking of himself, not for the reader's sake, but for self-love's sake. But of late he seems better to comprehend the essayist's proper subjectivity. We should not despair of essayists: no type of writer is rarer; the planets must conspire to make him; he must not be overwhelmed by life and drawn into other modes of expression.

Our generation has been lucky to possess one English essayist who has maintained and handed on the great tradition. I mean Stevenson. Although, in view of the extent and vogue of his novels and tales, Stevenson's essay work may seem almost an aside, it really is most significant. He is in the line of Charles Lamb. Where a man like Pater writes with elegance and suggestion after the manner of the suave and thoroughly equipped critic, Stevenson does a vastly higher thing; he talks ruddily, with infinite grace, humor, pathos and happiness, about the largest of all themes,—human nature. From "Ordered South" to "Pulvis et Umbra," through many a gay mood of smile and sunshine to the very deeps of life's weltering sea, Stevenson runs the gamut of fancy and emotion, the fantasticality of his themes being in itself the sign manual of a true essayist. In the Letters no man using English speech has chatted more unreservedly, and with more essential charm; it is the undress of literature that always instinctively stops this side of etiquette, of decency. The Stevenson epistles drive us on a still-hunt outside of the mother-tongue for their equal, with little prospect of quarry save within French borders.

The essay is thus a literary creature to the making of which go mood and form—and the former would seem by far the paramount thing. Great and special gifts does it demand. 'Tis an Ariel among literary kinds, shy, airy, tricksy, elusive, vanishing in the garish light that beats down upon the arena where the big prizes of fiction are competed for amidst noise, confusion and éclat. But ever in its own slight, winsome way does it compel attention and gain hearts for its very own. 'Tis an aristocrat of letters; nowhere is it so hard to hide obvious antecedents. Many try, but few triumph in it. Therefore, when a real essayist arrives, let him be received with due acclaim and thanks special, since through him is handed on so ancient and honorable a form.

THE MODERN NEED FOR LITERATURE *

In the childhood of nations the need for literature was the need for knowledge. Long before literature received its name or was associated with the printed page, imaginative utterance in epic, lyric, play or Saga had its utilitarian value, because through such forms history was handed down and popular wisdom embalmed. The minstrel chanted of battle almost before the warriors were breathed, their sinews relaxed; unwritten law, which is traditional custom, was framed in gnomic rhymes for the better remembering of the people; early ballads spread the amatory news of the countryside; later broadsides bruited the burning topics of the day in towns.

Even the Philistine could appreciate literature which conserved these practical aims. Few men deny the necessity of information: if so-called poetry can convey it, they are willing to tolerate colorful speech and the lure of rhythmic movement, however insensitive they may be to such charm. Moreover, it is only fair to the way-faring man, now or in the dawn of time, to represent him as not quite indifferent to picture-making and music in language. Humanity in mass en-

---

* An address for the Commencement Exercises at the Rush Medical College in Chicago, June 21st. 1901

joys a figure (though not recognizing and naming it after the manner of the rhetorics) ; and stands at gaze before a singer, even if the accompaniment be on a barrel-organ. It may well be believed that in the elder days when literature was thus a vehicle for the preservation and transmission of knowledge, many folk liked literature for its own sake. But letters (as we now call them) certainly had a solider standing on change aforetime because of this practical use, this close kinship with information.

With the development of society, however, has come a change. As civilization became articulate and complex, literature slowly, surely differentiated itself from the practical and utilitarian; and knowledge—science, to give it a familiar and restrictive name—stood forth clearly over against the imaginative expression of life, whether in art or letters. And when this happened, the Philistine no longer needed literature, nor liked it. He had an instinctive feeling that it was sham, make-believe, a lying about life· or a prettifying of life for the amusement of the idle rich. This view is of course of the Bœotian variety of thought; yet common enough of old, nor altogether departed this world even now. But as men waxed in civilization, in culture, they came gradually to see that literature in any worthy sense was something higher; that it could even be of better use than for the transmission of information or the killing of time; that it embraced within its

spacious domain all such records and accounts of
human beings and their actions as should give us
a sense of the power, beauty, grandeur and terror
of life so that its true significance might be
grasped. Literature in the enlightened modern
view is an interpretation of life both as fact and
as symbol; not only in terms of number and space
and time-sequence, but in terms of heart and soul
as well—in terms of living.

If this be true, we need not hold back from de-
claring that literature is one of the world's great
mouthpieces for the expression of ideals. To say
this is not to ignore the pleasure-giving province
of letters; the pleasure being, nevertheless, a
means to an end rather than the end itself; just
as Emerson shows how love between the young
man and maiden, that divine prologue to the
human drama which seems the play itself, is in
reality but a step to lead those dear young
creatures on to a final comprehension of the
spiritual love in the universe—or, as the theo-
logian would put it, to a knowledge of God.
There is nothing, I say, in this conception of literature hostile to the idea of amusement, pleasure,
that inheres in it. Indeed that is literature's way
of doing good; and the degree of joy that is got
out of a book is a measure of its fruitfulness for
us. Too often the province of instruction and
the province of pleasure in literature are contrasted as if they were antithetical, which is the
veriest nonsense. Instruction in the noblest sense

can come only where there is antecedent pleasure.
Witness the school-child beginning to stir within
and to grow, simply because he or she suddenly,
unexpectedly, finds a lesson interesting—because
it seems in some way related to life as the boy
or girl knows life; or as it has been warmed by the
magnetism of a real teacher—not a text-book with
arms and legs.

Literature and religion, along with the arts,
are the chief sources for the supplying of ideals.
And whereas religion has an immense advantage in
authority and gravity of aim, it is hardly too much
to say for literature that in its secularity as well
as in its plastic power to embrace the human case
in all conceivable varieties, there lies a certain
leverage; while in the fact that literature teaches
not didactically but by the winsome indirection
of art, there is an obvious added strength,—the
soul of mankind being caught unawares, as it
were, through sensitiveness to beauty, by the
spirit of good which is in literature—and in life.
Matthew Arnold, you will remember, went so far
as to assert his belief that all that should be retained of the religion of the future would be its
essential poetry, the husks of form, the shards of
dogma, being dropped behind. In other words, he
thought that literature would swallow up religion.
Without acting upon so radical a prophecy, surely
we may feel that great literature in its enlighten-
ment and uplift is always a handmaid of true religion, trying to do much the same for man in a

somewhat different way; approaching the one
Temple by another avenue, the avenue of Beauty
instead of by the avenue of the Good, both meeting in the avenue of the True, which runs straight
on and into the Holy of Holies—for the Temple
is one.

Every age, then, needs its ideals, since they are
magnets pointing the polar paths of conduct, of
righteousness; touchstones of character; lamps to
the feet of those who would walk upon the mountains. And literature, defined with any adequacy,
can do a vast deal to create and hand on these
ideals. In this sense, mankind's need for literature is permanent.

Perhaps some one thinks I do not allow sufficiently for the lower grades of what is called
literature. We cannot always be on the heights.
Moreover,

> "Not always the air that is rarest
> Is fairest,
> And we long in the valley to follow
> Apollo,"

complains the poet. There is neutral ground
where books furnish us pleasure or pastime but
fail of the great things here claimed for them.
Granted. There are foot-hills and intermediate
slopes as well as shining peaks; in fact, the
humbler altitudes are the condition of having
mountains at all. Yet, when we say mountains,
we mean, rightly enough, the aerial summits,
the aeries of eagles, topped by virginal snows,

seeming inaccessible to common mortals. And likewise, when we speak of literature and would discover its true physiognomy, we very properly emphasize the lofty creations which are to be seen from afar and lift themselves nearest to God.

But our day, it seems to me, has a special need for the inspiration from literature—from great essay, fiction, drama and poetry—and for particular reasons. Ours is a complex and cosmopolitan time; hence, literature can do not one but a number of services for it, corresponding to the symptomatic phases of the age. The present era is called carelessly this or that: material, on the hunt for Yankee inventions; commercial, on the hunt for the dollar; scientific, on the hunt for the fact; spiritual, on the hunt for psychic phenomena and for strange new gods; agnostic, rejoicing in the cry, "There is no God and August Compte is His Prophet;" decadent, out-heroding Herod in obscene rites; humanitarian, seeking to play the part of the good Samaritan as never before. The truth is we are none of these exclusively, but all of them, and more too. It takes a wide vision to cover such a time as this; it is a narrow, anemic view which interprets the Zeitgeist as if it were a one-theory movement. Let us have a look at a few of these streams of tendency, to see how they offer literature her opportunity.

We are scientific, I say. We study objective phenomena as they have never been studied before.

How august the revealments of the nineteenth century in this vast field of research! To read a book like Wallace's "The Wonderful Century," or John Fiske's "A Century of Science" is as stimulating to the imagination as an Arabian Nights Entertainment. You, gentlemen of the graduating class, find it your privilege to enter on this noble quest of facts which shall effect the alleviation of suffering mankind and bring earth nearer to heaven,—yea, which in the far reaches of time may, it would almost seem to the quickened fancy, solve the riddle of immortality by the prolongation of human life, approximating ever to the limitless life of the Better Land. You are the prophets of Euthanasia, the bringers-in of hope. But this privilege of yours, this tireless hunt for cause and effect within the sphere of the psychophysical, is also your penalty, or may be. From very devotion to the fact, the spirit may be neglected; and a sort of atrophy of the nature result towards the things of the heart and imagination. This is not inevitable, of course; but it is a possible danger, especially to the scientist, pure and simple, who lacks the magnificent corrective which the good physician has in his daily practical ministrations to woful men and women. You remember Darwin's testimony: how, loving Shakspere and the major poets and fictionists, but obliged to turn his back upon literature for years because of stress of work, he found, to his astonishment, upon returning to those once-cherished friends, that a distaste for them had grown up in him—a remarkable example of the shrinking of a faculty through disuse. The scientific man, as perhaps no other, needs literature; not only as a legitimate amusement, a form of recreation—and we forget at times when we despitefully regard recreation that it means recreation—but also as an exercise of the soul, a stimulator of the emotive, intuitional, affectional and aspirational fibres of a person.

The patronizing, half-contemptuous attitude of the so-called practical person towards literature is sometimes a little hard to bear. A novel is to him something to let down on after dinner, along with the post-prandial cigar, turning away from real and important matters. People drop into poetry, as did Silas Wegg of blessed memory—'tis a weakness at the best. The drama affords horse-play, slang, the ballet and dubious situations, to jaded nerves and drooping spirits. There is in a single-eyed devotion to objective fact, to the realities of the senses, at least a possibility that an absurd under-valuation of literature may follow; its true dignity and significance being utterly lost sight of in such a topsy-turvy notion of the relations of things in life that the first may be last and soul be as nothing to flesh. Literature in the high sense is a wholesome antidote for that particular form of Philistinism which harps tiresomely upon what is known as the practical,— utility and the like, meaning that which can be felt, touched, tasted and seen. To the philosopher, all is practical which advances the race, and that most practical which most helps the highest in man; and all is useful which best considers man's highest uses. This wretchedly limited, purblind, market-place conception of life cannot be held by one who enters sympathetically into the privileges of literature. And, when fact in this special and narrow sense is emphasized (as it is in our new century), it is a blessed thing that a door still stands invitingly open upon a garden of delights, upon the pleasances of the imagination, fairer, richer than ever before, so notable have been the additions to the garden-growths during the past one hundred years—that wonderful nineteenth century literature, fruit of so many lands and kinds.

Again, ours is a day when the dollar is believed to be mighty, if not almighty! the multi-millionaire is a type of manhood emblazoned in newspaper and magazine, all but worshiped at the family altar. By no means is the American unique here; but viewing modern life broadly, is it not true that there is an increasing tendency to grade people by their bank-account, to give a new meaning to the word idolatry? Now, literature, when true to its mission, reflects and interprets life (its raw material) in such wise that no such disproportionate estimate of money is possible; simply because in a broad, sane outlook on life, money is shown to be but a means to an end,—

and that end the realization in each and all of us
of our potentialities, so that a happier, richer and
higher life shall ensue and society at large be
permanently benefited. The voice of all literature
is consentient in thus acclaiming the real meaning of life; to wit, character-formation, growth
towards the ideal for ourselves and others. Its
teaching is all that way,—just as truly when it
exhibits vice, degradation and despair as when
sailing majestically upon the winds of heaven
high above human frailty. For in sounding the
dissonance, literature makes us to yearn for the
celestial harmonies; we would not recognize the
discordant as such, in sooth, were it not for our
instinct for the great concords beneath the surface jars. Literature is all the while telling us
of life so that we read plain its obscure scroll,
understand its true values, and so are safeguarded
from the terribly shriveling idea of existence possible to the mere money grabber. After all, there
is something in the world, as Stevenson has it,
besides "mud and old iron, cheap desires and
cheap fears." George Eliot draws a Silas Marner,
and we see that hideous thing a miser weaned from
gold coin by the softer, tenderer gold of a lovely
little maiden's hair. Moliere paints a Harpagon,
and we shudder away from the possibility of that
same soulless passion. Dickens puts before us in
full length the elder Dombey that we may behold
the final melting of that man of marble to whom
business was a God, he being led by the potent

hand of his girl-child back to the real life he had so forgotten—the life of the simple affections and of household hearts. And Balzac's Grandet bites into our memory forever the awful consequences of that insatiable money-lust, with its demoniac power of warping man's nobler nature. Literature of the first order is always doing just this, I repeat; passing a healing hand across the eyes sealed by worldliness and making them to see, not through a glass darkly, but face to face. The need for literature is doubled whenever and wherever men and women are in bondage to these eidola of the world, the flesh and the devil.

But we are practical in the United States and need literature, again, because we incline to laud use rather than beauty—as if beauty were aught but a higher usefulness. We are a practical folk, it is said—which is on the whole a misleading generalization. Still, it is not to be denied that we are only of late beginning to turn from a strenuous attention to material and immediate interests, giving heed to higher interests. The Prince of Peace and Prosperity is the proper person to arouse the Sleeping Beauty from her slumber. There is here no matter for reproach; our problems during the century of the Republic have been practical; problems of Government, National, State and Municipal; problems economic and political. Arts and letters must of necessity wait on such work; the wonder is (in view of the situation) that Americans can point to such writers as distinguish and adorn the century just closed.

Our literary art, our architecture, public and private, our endeavors in music and painting, have all testified in the past to this necessary devotion to practical pursuits and services. But worthy accomplishment in these high activities is now common. The Exposition year of 1893 was a signal that we had in many ways stepped from our leading strings; and more and more with the growth of a leisured class shall we realize that immunity from wage-earning does not inevitably mean dissipation nor exclusive devotion to sports and society. While, with the establishment of a firm material basis for the cultivation of the higher faculties, literature, along with the other arts, should make its appeal to a constantly growing audience. And I believe it is doing so, the popular magazine, unjustly sneered at by some, being a sort of middle member in a chain which begins with the newspaper and ends with standard literature. If, along with steadily waxing material prosperity, there come not a corresponding response to such an art and revealer of life as literature, sorry will be our case indeed. That way decadence lies. A cultivation of the sense of beauty and the sense of righteousness (which are not twain, but one, the holiness of beauty, in Lanier's phrase, being as precious as the beauty of holiness) must go with general prosperity; otherwise, that land is doomed. All history is a sole trumpet-voice announcing these tidings.

The commonest mistake about literature is the notion that it is merely an ornament to life. The reason that a nation in the more practical period of its development has less to do with the arts is not because the time for luxury has not come; but because it is in a lower stage of evolution, and not altogether ready for the finer things, for a philosophic conception of the universe. Our best American literature, that made by the prophet sages and singers of New England, was produced under conditions giving the lie direct to the idea that only an environment of luxury begets creative works. The high thinking of an Emerson comes out of plain living.

But again, we need literature to idealize the conventional, the commonplace and the homely in life. I do not mean by idealize to falsify or sentimentalize; but to show the idea inhering in the gross and seemingly meaningless mass, to detach the symbol from the fact, so that the fact takes on significance and loveliness. Realism of the right sort should serve as a sort of gloss on the poet's text,

> "Flesh is as nothing to Spirit,
> And the essence of life is divine."

It should make apparent that as there is nothing harder so there is nothing higher than the daily doing of little duties; as Wordsworth calls them,

> "The little nameless unremembered acts
> Of kindness and of love."

It should show that war, which often seems but a huddle of carnage, a blaze of savage passions, is at least linked with the love of country, with the thought that "sweet and glorious it is to die for one's land;" that religion is something more than an observance of forms, being the merging of all lesser loves in the love of the Eternal Maker and Father; that even machinery has poetry in it, as Kipling's McAndrews has demonstrated. It is thus that literature should make a glory out of the grey substance of our days. This handling of the homely so that it is seen to have a touch of the heavenly, is the mission of your true realist. The great makers of literature are always in this sense realists as much as idealists. It is the way of Homer, of Dante, of Shakspere, of Cervantes; of Moliere, Goethe, Tolstoy, Meredith and Stevenson. Let me give an example from Master William Shakspere—master alike of human speech and human life; that inimitable scene in "Henry V," where from the mouths of his boon companions, Dame Quickly, Pistol, Nym, and Bardolph, we learn of the passing of Falstaff.

Sir John's death being announced by Ancient Pistol, says Bardolph, eyes ashine for the nonce as well as nose:

"Would I were with him, wheresoever he is, either in heaven or hell." What a world of good fellowship in that line! And then mine hostess goes on, with exquisite pathos, all unconscious and homely as it is:

"Nay, sure, he's not in hell; he's in Arthur's
bosom, if ever man went to Arthur's bosom." She
meant Abraham's bosom—but we are glad of the
slip, for emotion is always making slips of that
kind. "A' made a finer end and went away as
it had been any Christom child; a' parted even
just between twelve and one, even at the turning
o' the tide." You remember that Barkis, too, went
out with the tide in another great homely-life
scene: "For after I saw him fumble with the
sheets and play with flowers and smile upon his
fingers' ends, I knew there was but one way," (you
can hear the good dame snuffle by this time as she
continues) "for his nose was as sharp as a pen
and a' babbled of green fields." That sorry old
worldling, Falstaff, that fellow of sack and women,
thievery and braggadocio, being Christian reared,
does when he comes to the mind-wandering
which preludes death, revert to that most idyllic-
ally beautiful of psalms and is led beside still
waters, yea, lies down in green pastures, as if he
were a care-free boy again untouched of sin. Perhaps even he can say, "I will fear no evil, for thou
art with me." But hear Dame Quickly again:

"How now, Sir John! quoth I; what man, be
o' good cheer. So a' cried out, God, God, God!
three or four times. Now I, to comfort him, bid
him a' should not think of God; I hoped there was
no need to trouble himself with any such thoughts
yet. So a' bade me lay more clothes on his feet;
I put my hand into the bed and felt them, and

they were as cold as any stone; then I felt to the knees, and they were as cold as any stone; and so upward and upward, and all was as cold as any stone."

How circumstantial it all is, like a doctor's report for detail and accuracy; but how it is illuminated with a splendidly fraternal tolerancy towards all seamy humanity, living and dead. Of a sudden we realize that even the great confraternity of rogues—epitomized in this master-rogue of all literature—is united to us in a common bond of brotherhood; and that is a lesson worth while. Behold, I say again, the true and only realism. Is it too much to claim for literature that she has no mean mission in thus revealing a spirit of good in things counted evil, in suggesting that nothing is common and unclean past redemption? Such at least is the divine unwisdom of the pure in heart.

And now a message of literature for our time which I would especially bear down on is its power to help the agnostic mood. Never before, I must think, has a more gracious or a grander opportunity offered itself to literature than in this regard. Our generation has experienced a tremendous readjustment of ethical ideas, a veritable seismic upheaval, of which the tremors and rumblings have scarcely died away. The agnostic state of mind has been the natural outcome of all this change—which in the end will be seen to stand for gain more than loss. Now the essence

of great literature, like that of true religion, is of
a potency to furnish the doubting Thomases with
sweetness and light; with hope, inspiration and a
golden comfort: and it can do this with all the
winning gentleness of love and with that strength
of purity which is as the strength of ten. Agnosti-
cism is a brain state; literature appeals primarily
to the heart and is the antidote needed, offering
its warm-blooded, wholesome, imperative yea to
the cold analytic nay of the intellect. A very important function of literature in respect of modern
life lies here.

You are very well aware, however, that much
of current literature, so far from counteracting
this tendency to doubt and despair, abets it, and,
in fact, issues out of it. This is to be expected,
for literature (when honest) should always faith-
fully reflect the spirit of the Time; it is its duty
its privilege. Nor must we deny the benefit of
literature which not only mirrors the comparatively smooth surface waters of society but also
drops a plummet line into its murky abysmal
depths. The knife of the surgeon seeking to ex-
tirpate the root trouble is kindly meant and welcome.

Particularly is the literature which reveals the
predicaments of the weak, the wretched, the out-
cast of the earth, a serviceable addition to the
library table. There is a need of books that
awaken our sympathies for the under dog in the
social struggle, and make us to understand his

situation. The under dog will be dustier and perhaps bloodier than his conqueror and so is likely
to be less pleasant to look upon; but it were a sad
mistake not to pay attention to him. Never has
there been so much fiction and drama and poetry
that has expressed the

"Still sad music of humanity,"

and one deadens one's sensibilities and makes shallow one's nature in turning away from such books
simply because they are not agreeable. This spirit
extends even to animals. Nevertheless, I think we
can say, and say with emphasis, that in consideration of the liberal doses of pessimism furnished
for the past decade in the literature of civilized
lands, in view of the fact (already adumbrated)
that a more cheerful view of the world is becoming
popular, and with the additional consideration
that helpfulness and good cheer are prime merits
always in literary creations, we can say, I repeat,
that the paramount need just now is for books
that incite to courageous action, to high heart
and hope, to such a broad re-statement of the everlasting beautiful as shall make for happy living,
for vigorous deeds, for an outdoor optimism.

Of desiccated analytics, of dark psychic tortuosi-
ties, of eloquent variations on the overworked
theme, *vanitas vanitatum,* we have had enough
and to spare. The gospel for an age of doubt (to
borrow Dr. Van Dyke's name for it) should be of
gladder tidings. Modern literature must be thera-
peutic; it must carry healing in its wings. It

must not be a literature for and by mattoids. Nor
is this to slight the work of writers like Tolstoy,
Zola, Hardy, and Ibsen; we need them, too—and
have had them. But in the light of the tendency
for the past twenty years, and looking to the future, we need the literature of encouragement
more. How are we going to get it? It lies with
the thoughtful reading public; it can be effected
if that body of folk will show plainly in what they
buy, what sort of literature they prefer. The test
of sales is obvious and irresistible in its results.
If the great majority of those who support literature wish for the literature of encouragement
rather than for the literature of despair, and will
leave the one and cleave unto the other, the battle is won. It is a pity we cannot consciously
combine on this. Ours is an age of Trusts. I
should like to see a Trust of the Amalgamated
Interests of Consumers of the Literature of Ozone
and Sunlight, Unlimited. The title is rather cumbersome; but what a power-house that plant could
command.

In a word, and finally, literature is always
needed to be a spokesman of those deep-lying,
ever abiding instincts and affirmations of the soul
of man which dominate his life and shape his end.
And literature is of particular use to-day just in
proportion as we forget that life is more in the
spirit than in the flesh; that in order to any full
living, we must feed not the body only but the
mind and soul as well.

PAST AND PRESENT IN LITERATURE

The Bishop of London is credited with advising some young women students to read three books written before the year 1800 for every one written later. He declared that, in accordance with a vow, he had followed this plan for ten years and that those years had been the happiest of his life.

I hope his lordship said nothing of the sort; if he did, one is inclined to feel the more sympathetic toward Sydney Smith's remark—that famous wit had in mind the exceeding difficulty of turning the classic of a literature into the tongue of another—that everything suffers by translation —except a bishop.

For the imputed statement is foolish and misleading. It is an example of an often recurrent attitude toward the past and the present, the deification of the one and the depreciation of the other, so that great injustice is done to modern things. Deep in the human heart is implanted the yearning back toward a Golden Age, forward, to the Millennium; and the poor tarnished present pays the penalty of its humdrum nearness, its unideal reality. It would be much closer to the truth to say that three books to one in favor of the nineteenth century were advisable, especially if the literature of the English-speaking race be in mind; and the bishop's words, as reported, would seem to have meant that. Think for a moment what such a dictum implies! It belittles, or at least throws out of proportion, the poetry of Keats, Shelley and Byron, of Wordsworth and Coleridge, of Browning, Tennyson and Swinburne, of Poe, Whitman and Kipling, the romances and novels of Scott, Hawthorne and Stevenson, of Eliot, Dickens and Thackeray, of later men and women like Meredith, Hardy, Ward and Barrie; it slights the essay work of Lamb, Hunt, Hazlitt, De Quincey and Irving, of Carlyle and Ruskin, of Emerson and Lowell. These and many others scarcely less worthy are set aside, by implication, as if in writing later than that arbitrary mark of 1800 they had committed the unpardonable sin. I am running over, be it observed, but a few stellar names, and am confined to authors using our own tongue. If continental literature were to be included, the bishop's offense becomes more heinous, for one's head fairly buzzes with the great creative writers whose labor has since been done.

In short, taking the range, variety and quality of performance and the number of representatives into the consideration, the simple fact is that no century in the whole evolution of our magnificent English literature is so rich and worthy of laud as the one just closed, not even Shakspere's, on the principle that one swallow does not make a summer. It is the part of common-sense, justice and patriotism to say this; the danger in twisting the truth into an undue exaltation of the by-gone —fine as that may be—is the neglect of the present-day literature by those who are likely to be led by what to them seems a final judgment, to wit, the opinion of a bishop.

There is a special reason why the present in literature should be appreciated at its full worth. The very fact that it *is* the present, not the past, is in its favor. Even if nineteenth century literature were distinctly inferior to the eighteenth, instead of being triumphantly greater, it would be ill-advised to undervalue the former; nay, it would still have an interest for us beyond that of any other time. And this, simply because it represents our day. Literature always reflects life, and the best literature of a given age is a mirror in which we may see move the body of the age, and, listening, catch the sound of its heart-beats. Its language is our own; it expresses our ideals, industrial, social, political, philosophical, spiritual; it involves a hundred questions pertinent to our own period and to no other, perhaps not yet born in 1800. This side of literature is, to be sure, in large measure its practical and intellectual side, its contribution to knowledge, having less to do with the æsthetic denotements of charm and beauty. But these æsthetic conceptions themselves also change. The ideal of beauty is by no means eternal. A representative piece of literature during the past fifty years, or thirty years, is a sure registration of this shift of both thought and feeling.

To give an illustration: The rise and spread of the doctrine of evolution since 1850 is the century's mighty contribution to science; all literature since 1850, beginning with such a masterpiece as Tennyson's "In Memoriam," feels this change, reflects the revolution of thought that is involved. To read literature before 1800, to the neglect of that written in the second half of the century just closed, is to be hopelessly out of touch with all modern thinking, to show oneself an intellectual *fainéant*. This is an illustration having in mind literature as intellectual pabulum, as mind-stuff. But take literature as art, too: Since realism so-called became the dominant creed, beauty, the aim of all art, has come to be regarded as something different from the older conception; not as the antithesis to truth, not a prettification of fact or a falsification thereof, but a more forcible presentation of truth itself. Hence, in the books that do not flinch in setting down the dark and terrible in human life, we recognize a kind of beauty—"the still, sad music of humanity." Thus the notion of art itself has widened, I say; our idea of the province of the æsthetic has been stretched to admit more of life, of reality. And it is only in the literature of the last half-century that this fruitful lesson has been learned; to turn away from its lesson is mentally to stunt oneself.

It is our first business to know and believe in the present, upon the firm basis of a thorough culture in all the past has to offer. But the past should be studied for the sake of the present, not vice versa; nor, worse yet, by a grudging concession made to the Now in the reading of one book to the prescribed three of an earlier time. I am convinced that the temper of mind personified in the Bishop of London comes of a false worship of outgrown gods. An old man fondly idealizes the days of his own youth, whereas, when they were being lived in, he grumbled over them right heartily. In the same way, some people grow all but maudlin over a past age which, were it the present, they would be the first to satirize. If (which God forbid!) we could reverse Time's dial and be set down in the past, to wrestle with all its enormities, we should then find (if we doubted it before) that the world is moving forward, not backward, and that literature has responded to this general law. It is this wholesome truth which Mark Twain inculcates in his "A Connecticut Yankee in King Arthur's Court," as serious a book as was ever writ.

Nor is this view to disparage the literary past; to deny that it is rich in writers who can teach and delight us—spirits who still rule us from their urns: Chaucer's charm of musical narrative and homely delineation; Spenser's linked sweetness, as he cries up chivalric deeds; Shakspere and his fellows and soon-followers, forming the golden

time of letters; the seventeenth century with its
great central figure of Dryden; the early eighteenth, with Addison, Steele, and Swift; the middle years, bringing that wonderful new birth, the
novel, in the hands of Richardson, Fielding, and
Smollett; the second half, with Johnson, Goldsmith, and the rest. Even to run thus over the
names of a few mountain peaks, where the foot-
hills and valleys hide humbler scenes which yet
yield us everlasting joy, is to kindle the enthusiasm of the sincere lover of English literature.
To read and know and love those earlier authors
is not only to add to our stock of permanent pleasure; it is to be instructed in the development of
the English race, since in its literature a race is
best, because most spontaneously, reflected. The
finest literature of a period is always the truest
exponent of that time, since it is by his ideals that
we properly judge the aspiring creature called
man. The high-water mark on the beach alone
registers the tide; all lower wave impulses are
obliterated.

Then, too, there is—and rightly—an illusion
of the past which lends a fascination to older
literature, and many are drawn to it for that reason. This attraction is in response to what may
be called the human instinct for romance; seen
just now in the general turning to historical fiction. The quaintness, unwonted color, and heroic
proportions assumed by what is remote in time
help to produce this well-nigh thaumaturgic effect,

an effect most enjoyable and, within proper limits, perfectly legitimate.

But all possible concessions being made, it remains true that the disproportionate estimate of the literary past in contrast with the present—as exampled in the statement attributed, I hope erroneously, to the Bishop of London—is a form of affectation or ignorance which should be met with candid hostility whencesoever it comes. The student should be reared to a reverential admiration for the literary riches of the last one hundred years, which it is his privilege to be born into; the lover of books should, in the very light of his knowledge of the past, come to a fuller appreciation of the glories of a later day. And the critic should be constantly on guard against the insidious danger of an unbalanced admiration for some pet school or author or period, lest his sense of relative values —so essential to any real criticism—be lost and he fall into the habit of belittling the larger and overpraising that which is of less moment. Young folk, as a rule, have a natural and healthy interest in the present—including the literary present. They are pretty likely to read current books rather than those which are older. Therefore, it is probable that the Bishop's sort of suggestion, made to college students, would be comparatively innocuous. But those same young folk, when they come to maturity, might act in accordance with the advice; might even take to heart Charles Lamb's whimsical saying, that whenever a new volume

appeared he read an old one. And if the habit
of regarding contemporaneous literature with suspicion were thus formed, the result would be an
unhappy one. A belief in the present, whether it
be literature or life which makes literature possible, is, when you come to think of it, a belief
in the great laws and unfolding potentialities of
the universe. Life greatens toward the light, and
the nineteenth century is the heir of the ages.
Let us rejoice in it.

THE USE OF ENGLISH

If the study of the English language in its uses
and abuses seem dry and repellent, it is, I must
think, the fault of the pedant who handles it.
Few things are of more general interest to those
who use English speech—and what a vast army
they make—than the manipulation of the mother
tongue in its manifold meanings. We all use English whether we will or no; alas, how many of
us misuse it! To be sure, one may be born into
English, grow up, love, pay taxes, and be buried
in it, with the same unconsciousness of its privileges and demands as that displayed by M. Jour-
dain with regard to the use of prose. Still, to all
who enjoyed the advantages of some schooling, the
right uses of this linguistic opportunity is not a
matter of indifference. The great majority of
English speakers and writers come to a conscious
love of the language. It is a thing inwrought with
their life and the life of others near and dear. No
language is a dead thing, though the dry scientific
analysis of scholars lead wrongly to that opinion.
Rather, is each a mighty store-house of human
treasures; a musical instrument, listening to which
one may hear an infinitude of melodies. Men
have for centuries laughed and loved in it, sworn
and been forsworn, hated and hoped, yea, lived

and died.   No wonder if it be a symphonic creature, full of crashing harmonies, of the caresses
of poetry, of tumultuous discords, and of divine
songs of peace.

If this be true of any tongue, it is emphatically
true of a dominant tongue like the English—
native in so many lands, spoken under so many
skies, so militant in its march, so plastic in its
manifold adaptations to the needs of its children.
It is a tongue made splendid by more than a thousand years of great literature.   It is the home
speech of more folk than those who make populous
the shores of Kipling's seven seas.   The history
of words and of the sentences into which they
fall, is no dry record of bloodless facts, but as
dramatic as the history of mankind; indeed, it is
the history of man as he has crystallized into a
sound-symbol the thoughts, imaginings, faiths
and aspirations of his life, from the cave dwellers
to the Darwin of his century.   Words, like men,
have their "strange, eventful histories," and, again
like men, one word in its time "plays many parts."
To follow the ups and downs of a single proper
noun—a stupid name since its career is as often
as not improper and hence doubly fascinating—or
of a common noun—named with equal stupidity,
since its story is likely to be most uncommon—this
pursuit, I say, is often as exciting as a novel or a
foot-ball game.   Thus it follows that the dictionary (rightly used and comprehended) is the most
interesting of all books, save perhaps the Bible.

Dr. Holmes knew this when he made the Auto-crat say: "When I feel inclined to read poetry I take down my dictionary. The poetry of words is quite as beautiful as that of sentences. The author may arrange the gems effectively, but their shape and luster have been given by the attrition of ages. Bring me the finest simile from the whole range of imaginative writing, and I will show you a single word which conveys a more profound, a more accurate, and a more eloquent analogy." Emerson had the same feeling when he wrote: "It does not need that a poem should be long. Every word was once a poem."

As a matter of personal testimony, I may say that I never open a dictionary without a conscious quiver of excitement at the likelihood of a sensational experience. It is almost a miracle that such a study has had the power of converting living men (scholars, in the ordinary parlance) into dry-asdusts. One would suppose it might have an effect analogous to that of earth-contact upon Antæus. I dare say it is because they have studied the bones, not the flesh and blood of language, making themselves scientists instead of amateurs of life. For language, in reality, is a manifestation of life, and always that. The dead languages, we say, meaning the people are dead who spoke them; which is no fault of the tongue itself, which lives lustily on in its literature.

It will do no harm, now, to illustrate the statement as to the essential poetry, pathos and drama inherent in these vital word-symbols. And first, a striking example of the rise and fall of the same word. The noun *cwen* in Old English had the generic significance of "woman," with no reference to station or moral status. In the course of time, and with a modified spelling, it appeared tricked out as our modern English *queen,* a sovereign of the people—the highest earthly lot attainable by the sex. And yet, in another dress of letters— for spelling has played a part in the drama of words like to that played by clothes among humanity—it paraded itself in Elizabethan times and still lives as *quean,*—a common drab, a painted woman of the town! These two words from the selfsame ancestor, differentiated by a garb of letters, run the gamut of woman's social and moral possibilities. Surely nothing could be more impressive; a single noun, yet a whole sermon on sex!

Think, too, how personal names lend themselves to picturesque effects. Duns Scotus was in the thirteenth century a great scholar, the last of the great schoolmen; but, like other great men before and since, he had enemies, who called him unpleasant epithets and jeered at his philosophy, until his nick-name Duns became with them a term of reproach and ridicule. And behold! we say "dunce" to-day to the stupid schoolboy who wears the conical cap in the corner. The wisest man of his time gives the tongue its stock designation for a fool! It were well for dunces to realize how honorable a pedigree they boast of. Let me illustrate once more. Dickens in his "Tale of Two Cities" speaks of the "figure of that sharp female called La Guillotine." There is a popular notion abroad that Dr. Guillotin was the inventor of that terrible machine whose maw was fed with such drastic food during the red days of the Terror in France the unfortunate. But as a matter of fact, to one Dr. Louis belongs the dubious honor of the invention. Guillotin was a man of mercy who in the very year of the outbreak of the French Revolution advocated the abolition of this grim method of capital punishment. And the people, forsooth, with tremendous irony, set his blameless name upon an instrument of extermination which bears in the minds of men a bad eminence, like Milton's Satan. The sardonic satire of history has few more striking examples.

These instances of the weatherings of words typify a host more, and may serve to illuminate my thesis that all that man has thought and felt is registered in language, which therefore offers a study of widest scope and of thrilling interest.

It seems an ironic comment upon the inutility of education that language, in proportion as it becomes learned, grows colorless, abstract, formal, and unexciting. The speech of the philosopher is not only hard to be understood by the people, but seemingly stripped of all life and color, whereas the talk of the huckster on the street, the craftsman in the shop, or the sailor on the sea has a smack, an

idiosyncrasy, that makes it relishable. Their
words are at once concrete and imaginative. Yet,
since all language roots in metaphor, the abstruse
lingo of a Kant was once of imagination all com-
pact. The palest word-medium of to-day is the
metaphor of by-gone years; the most brilliant pic-
ture-coin of the present will become the outworn
counter of the future. Language when handled
by children is instructive, for a child in this regard stands for the youth of the race. We commonly speak of the little folk as unconscious poets
and for this very reason: they talk in tropes, their
fancies are expressed in figures. As the analytic
processes of maturity gain on the intuitive, creative acts of speech, this imaginative element slowly disappears, until it is only the grown-up
poet (who in this respect preserves his childlike-
ness) that dares to use language in an unconventional way,—in which use he is joined, however,
by the unlettered all about, whose conversation,
being offhand and instinctive, and being, moreover, vitally related to their interests and occupa-
tions, has the savor of real things and a certain
fresh felicity. It is also instructive to see how,
with all of us, our speech is happy when we are
most at ease and hence most natural; the drawing-
room garb and the drawing-room idiom are alike
drearily limited. The same people who in the
street or at their business will be racy of speech,
wax jejune and uninspiring under the social
lamps. Evening dress seems to throttle idiom.

This leads us to a plain fact as to the origin of language: it is the birth of instinct, of emotion, of imagination; not a reasoned-out process but a creative impulse; a blundering yet puissant effort of man's genius. Whatever our theory of the beginning of speech, this holds true. And it is a truth with a direct bearing upon all present-day questions of language-use—a veritable searchlight in the fog.

Granting, now, the attractions of this study, a remark must be made as to the certificate of authority in matters of language. Plain speaking is in place here. People discuss questions of speech-use with the same freedom with which they comment upon the weather; this is the immemorable parade ground of cock-sure judgments. Innumerable little friendly battles are fought upon this or that moot-point and there is a general feeling that one man is as good as another in the contest. This is all well enough for the innocuous tilts of society; but if the point at issue be taken seriously, it is well to remember that in this subject, as in all others, the specialists must decide. No person of culture familiar with the present-day uses of English, but lacking knowledge of the tongue in its historical development, is in a position to lay down the law. This is why many popular books upon words and their uses are often misleading and darken counsel. These authors may be intelligent, they may have considerable acquaintance with current linguistic habits; but they are not philologists; and it is the language-student and he alone who is wise in the premises. In other spheres of human knowledge this principle is acted upon; it must be held to firmly here.

Many so-called vulgarisms may be explained if not excused by an appeal to the history of English words. The wayfaring man says "six year ago" and "six head of cattle," omitting the plural sign; the one expression would be called vulgar, the other vernacular, idiomatic. But both have historical ground; they look back to a time when the plural significance was indicated not by the addition of s, as in the modern speech, but by the genitive case, "six year" being in reality, in its older form "six of years" (Old English, *six geara*). And the instinct of idiom has preserved even to our own day this thousand-year-old fact. Again, in the analogous phrase "a six foot cable," we see exactly the same principle at work. It is more idiomatic still to give the old form. Imagine calling it a "six feet cable!" Yet even the keenly intelligent who discuss language on the basis of merely current usage will be forced for consistency's sake to favor that form of the phrase, although puzzled to find that, somehow, it quite lacks the right flavor.

In the same way, a knowledge of word lineage sheds light upon pronunciation. An examination of English literature from earliest times down to the present, teaches the student that a general law of accent is at work in our language. It may be called the radical tendency of our tongue in this matter; the tendency to move the accent back to the root syllable. A tendency at variance to this is that of euphony, which in polysyllabic words demands such distribution of emphasis as shall satisfy the ear; and in all words requires some attention to musical values. But this is minor to the major law of the backward-working accent. Foreign words introduced into our tongue, are at first pronounced after their native laws: but just in proportion as they become anglicised, do they fall under this rule, their accent receding towards the root or (in case the root and first syllable do not agree) to the first syllable of the word. Thus, in Marlowe's play, "The Jew of Malta," occurs the line:

And with extorting, cozening forfeit'ing,

where the accent of the last word must, to the best results of music, fall upon the second syllable: while to-day it has reached the first syllable, *for'-feiting*. The word being French, this earlier pronunciation is just what one would expect. Coming a hundred years nearer our own time, we find in Milton's "Paradise Lost" the line:

Their planetary motions and aspects'.

In this case, a Latin word is, in the seventeenth century, naturally, more conscious of its origin than is the case now, when, more thoroughly English, it receives the native accent *as'pects*.

Moving another hundred years toward the present time, in Thomas Grey's "Sketch of His Own Character" the opening lines run as follows:

Too poor for a bribe and too proud to impor'tune,
He had not the method for making a fortune.

Here, obviously, the end of the first line is made to rhyme with *fortune*. The present pronunciation of the word is, however, *im'portune'*; that is to say, it has moved back to the first syllable, with a secondary accent on the third. Robert Browning, with the older accentuation in mind, has ventured in one of his poems to use *impor'tune*.

The value of having this general principle clearly in mind is shown when it comes to be applied to certain words which at a given moment seem to be trembling in the balance between the older and the newer accent. Thus, *acces'sory* and *ac'cessory*; which? The latter, for the simple reason that that is the stress destined, by the law of recessive accent, to prevail.

Likewise, of *inqui'ry* and *in'quiry*, the last is preferable, for the same reason. It would be moving directly against a deep-lying linguistic law—a tendency inherent in the speech of the race—to try to make *inqui'ry* and *acces'sory* exclusive good use, at the expense of the later and better usage. As well might a child attempt to check a tidal wave. Current good usage must always be carefully observed; but without the corrective knowledge of facts lying behind the present show of things, it is a dangerous guide; it is the flower of which the historic life is the hidden but potent root.

Another and important service rendered by a thorough knowledge of English old and new, is that it develops a sensitiveness to the vernacular, and a liking for the native word, phrase, idiom. Simplicity, strength, and beauty in speech are appreciated above a quasi or questionable elegance. There is a deal of culture in that feeling for language which gives preference to the idiom *go to bed* over *to retire*. The former stands for a large class of plain, direct, homely expressions, too often avoided by the linguistically ill-educated. When one falls into conversation with a stranger, one may judge him infallibly by this test: a brief exchange of small talk reveals his station and degree with awful certainty—far more surely than do his dress and carriage. The habit of shoddy expression in speech when one is desirous of making a good impression is astonishingly prevalent. In sooth, it takes something of education to feel the full value of a vigorous simplicity of utterance. The taste for a sort of bastard Websterianism of speech for the purposes of ordinary conversation is, I fear, peculiarly American: a survival, too, of older conditions. Dickens satirizes this manner of talk in "Martin Chuzzlewit," unkindly, perhaps, but hardly untruly—for the year of grace 1842. It is less fashionable now, just as the old-time oratory is less fashionable, being supplanted by the terse, pithy, plain-spoken style of public utterance. In this matter of vernacular directness our cousins English have always set us a good example,—one we are slowly but surely learning to follow. In the past, there may have lurked in our minds a conviction that the free use of euphuistic, absurdly showy words for very simple things was a sign of the possession of *savoir faire:* as confidence grows along with experience, the speech clarifies and takes on a seemly plainness.

So inspiriting is it to hear truly idiomatic English—English with grip to it as well as grace—that the pleasure breeds leniency toward that abuse of idiom commonly called "slang." The relations of the two have scarcely been set forth to satisfaction.

The kinship of slang and idiom is very close. They are blood-relations. Indeed, it might almost be said that one is the other under a sobriquet. Slang is often but idiom in the making. The idiom of to-day was slang in Shakspere's time; and the slang of this year may become accredited idiom a century hence. Nevertheless, the word slang, together with such other words as dialect, patois, argot, and their like, has something of a sinister implication; and it will be well to examine the case to see if the popular feeling about it be justified.

Slang in the common meaning, is not only colloquial speech, but speech that is low, vulgar; any good dictionary definition supports this statement. Skeat, the authority in English etymology, derives the word, no doubt properly, from an ancient Scandinavian original which is seen in our verb *to sling*—so that when in our jocular American way we speak of "slinging language," we are going back to root flavors. Slang is language which is slung about recklessly, not to say profanely. It cannot be denied that some hard things are truthfully to be spoken in its disfavor. Some of it is gutter-born and naturally dies the death of all disreputable outcasts. A good deal of it falls from the lips of thieves, gypsies, tramps and other such motley classes of society, regarded for the most part as outside the pale of decency. An appreciable amount of it, at least, is obscure, because of an inadmissible technicality; and, worse still, is unimaginatively narrow and unpicturesque— qualities that condemn it to a short life, and preclude its having any life that is more than local and uncertain. I have sometimes thought in noting the informal dialect of college students that they should have been able to show better invention in their creation of a fraternal jargon; it lacks variety, verve, inspiration. It is but justice to them to say that sometimes they live up to their opportunity and are racily original. But there is a reason for the fact that a good share of the slang so called—perhaps half of whàt is widely current at a given moment—perishes and perishes deservedly. If one interested in this stimulating subject will take the trouble to register half a dozen of the prevalent slang expressions at a certain date and will then refer to them a couple of years thereafter, he will be instructed to his satisfaction in the ephemerality of much of this unconventional current idiom.

Yet this is only half the story. I implied as much in speaking of the inter-relations. Not all slang is bad: some of it is good, nay, delightful. It is created just as all living language is created —impulsively, with a certain joy in the creation, and at the call of the genuine need. It is an attempt at picturesqueness, liveliness, reality, and when it is not brought forth for too narrowly special a use nor by a parent morally debased, the slang word or expression is quite often acceptable. If this seems over-praise, conversion to the view will follow an examination of the facts. People are often shocked by a felicitous but unconventional idiom (which they call slang) not so much because their feelings are really outraged as because they imagine it is their duty to be shocked. It is a case of mock modesty; in their hearts there is a guilty enjoyment of such language. The real question is that of actual vulgarity; because the idiom is new or, what is taken to be the same thing, unknown, is no condemnation. This deeper-going question lies behind it: is the expression coarse, offensive to good taste, or out-and-out immoral? And to pronounce upon this is a very delicate test of one's knowledge of language, literature, even of life itself.

Now it is just the language-wielder with a feeling for idiom based upon a generous knowledge of English past and present, who is at once bold yet careful in his relation to slang, so called. Aware of the fact that slang is often excellent new idiom, he uses it with little fear of results; while he has, in his sensitiveness to what is truly good English, an all but infallible touchstone by which to detect the merely low and ephemeral. It follows that his language is delightfully free from pedantic stiffness or mawkish euphuism. It possesses the racy quality that is the very salt of speech, and a freedom that strikes prudes as audacious at times, yet has a felicity recognizable even by those who have neither the courage nor the education to go and do likewise. He prefers to handle the native vocabulary "After the use of the English in straight-flung words and few," as Kipling has it. He knows that the foreign elements of a tongue are for ornamentation or special application; that the vernacular is the back-bone.

It is in respect of such considerations that a study of English, an interest in the mother speech extending far beyond the days of formal schooling, commend themselves to all. There is an exhaustless attraction in it. Moreover, an assured comprehension of the subject is the best possible basis for all appreciation of our literature from Beowulf to Browning,—is, in fact, the only safe and sure substructure for any literary appreciation. One who begins the study of Chaucer, of Spenser or of Shakspere without this advantage, trips on the first page; it is inevitable. Thus the study of language and the study of literature, though unfortunately too much treated as if they were utterly apart, the one a science, the other an art, are in reality so closely co-ordinate as to be but phases of the one great subject; language the instrument, literature the alluring, the inspiriting, the multitudinous airs that can be played upon it.

A NOTE ON MODERN CRITICISM

Literary criticism has always been of two main kinds: the objective, which applies rules and believes in standards; the subjective, which, with less care for canons, gives freer play to personal impressions. Some of the later doyens of letters belong to the impressionistic school, but of old the weight of authority was with those who appealed to tradition. And there was an authority in this method, a stability and dignity in the judgments thus reached, which made them imposing, even admirable. Nisard summed up the creed in saying: "I could not love without preferring, and I could not prefer without doing injustice." The personal equation is here reduced to the vanishing point. Jeffrey, with his famous critique of Wordsworth, beginning, "This will never do," affords a fine example of the same thing. A nobler illustration is Matthew Arnold, whose appeal to comparisons and insistence on a standard are academic in the best sense. In the hands of such a man, objective criticism is discovered to be full of virtues. But with an older school—with Boileau in France, to name one leader—the danger was a stiffening into the mechanical, loss of breadth, and insensitiveness to an enlightened enjoyment as the ultimate test.

With Sainte-Beuve, however (still looking to France, the land of criticism, *par excellence),* came a change. Taine, Renan, younger men like Jules Lemaître, with all their personal variations, admit more of the subjective, see the subject through the color of their temperament; and of modern criticism as a whole it may be said that it has become autobiographical. The critic announces: "Gentlemen, I propose to talk of myself in relation to Shakspere, Racine, Pascal, Goethe." In some cases this is pushed to an absurd or offensive degree, until we get a parody on literary judgments. But Mr. William M. Payne, in his recent book, "Little Leaders," goes too far in his condemnation of the subjective test. Professor Trent, in a well-considered paper to be found in a still later volume of essays, views the matter more broadly when he points out the share of truth in both the objective and subjective methods. Many of our ablest and most charming writers favor it: Stevenson, for an Englishman (who isn't English), Howells, for an American. The advantages of the latter are obvious: appreciating the truth in *de gustibus,* the critic gives his opinion for what it is worth, tolerant of dispute or dissent. He becomes intimate with us: we are more likely to love him. In addition to stimulation in literature, we are having dealings with a strong, pleasing personality, perhaps. The gain here is all in the direction of life, savor, reality. On the other hand, a besetting sin of this method is lack of

culture. Any one can set up to write esoteric criticism. But when, as with M. Lemaître, there is
wide reading, an assimilation of the best models,
the issue, be it confessed, is delightful.

In all likelihood, the question will always be
debatable. The modern tendency, no doubt, leans
towards the subjective; individualism for the moment is paramount in literature. The pendulum
swings to that side of equilibrium. Personal preference is the starting-point of all honest enjoyment and appreciation of literature. To praise a
book because we think it ought to be praised, not
because we find it praiseworthy, is intellectual sui-
cide. Yet few of us wish to go so far as to deny
that literary art has some permanent laws and
standards. The slow consensus of the best opinion
(with some erratic individual variations) rallies
around the works which obey these laws and con-
form to these standards. To listen to the still,
small voice within, and yet to find a reason-for-
being in the voice of time and authority, that is
the delicate and difficult business of the serious-
minded critic. The present-day tendency alluded
to is an exaggeration, but, if an excess, it must be
wholesomer, truer than the other, earlier excess,
which stretched every literary creation upon the
narrow Procrustean bed of convention and judged
its size thereby.

To justify the modern tendency it must be
shown that the long-cherished dicta pronouncing
art a thing of rule and standard, of well-defined

laws and unsurpassable boundaries, are not founded upon fact; or at least, have been given undue prominence. The latter hits near to the truth. There is more argument for this thesis than at first appears. An illustrative analogy may be drawn from the sister art of music. Our conceptions of what is right and beautiful in the æsthetic tone-world are based upon the seven-note scale; but with the Chinese, for example, the five-note scale is the norm and starting point. Truly, it is a purely subjective process of reasoning to assert that good music necessarily derives from the seven-note scale. The ear of most modern peoples accepts that scale, and rejects that of the Mongolians as displeasing; *voila tout*. The whole development of European music on its technical side rests thus upon an assumption it would take more than the subtlest metaphysics of a schoolman to show to be anything but unproved. At the best, an appeal to the history of music might force us to concede that the western scale has given to the world richer results; that the civilized folk have adopted the octave while those semi-civilized or worse have invented the five-note or other scales. But who dare say that some scale of the future shall not produce music as superior to that made upon the seven-note idea as the latter is superior to the five-note? In other words, musical technique is bottomed upon an arbitrary standard and not upon eternal laws. It is relative, not absolute, in its nature. In the domain of ethics a similar substitution of relative

for absolute has been brought about. The conscience is still regarded as innate by conservative
thinkers who accept the sense of right and wrong
as directly God-given; but in the Spencerian view
it is explained as a matter of racial experience,
utilitarian in its origin. Latter-day psychology
inclines to this theory; and, as a result, it may be
found working in the philosophy of literature
and of æsthetics. This thought tendency when
transferred to literary criticism irresistibly leads
towards a more personal and less hide-bound interpretation of the phenomena of literature.

But this much may be said with certitude: The
individual sense of moral right and wrong may be
subject to a long historical evolution and may,
during that process, show constantly higher ideals;
yet, whatever the ideal—grotesque, incomplete,
immoral at a given time and place—once accepted,
moral health depends upon eschewing what is
deemed wrong and cleaving to what is deemed
right. So in literary art, the æsthetic sense and
the laws thereto conforming demand that the
artist obey an ideal of the beautiful. Disobey it,
and the art product becomes unæsthetic, lying beyond the province of art. This æsthetic ideal may,
however, shift or vary according to racial differ-
ences and those of time. Yes, it may even differ
(within limits) in the case of two cultured persons of the same race, place and day. But the
concurrent critical opinion of the human intelli-
gence directed upon the materials of literature

does insist upon some ideal, and in all periods
and lands bases appreciation of the artistic product upon the sense of pleasure. What pleases—
using pleasure in the broad sense to include that
which emotionally arouses—is within the pale,
what is not pleasing lies without. It is not enough
that a person be pleased—the individual artist or
amateur; there must be wide agreement in order
that the variables incidental to the personal equation be eliminated as far as possible. Subtracting
all discrepancies and variances of ideal, a residuum
is left which declares for the ever clarifying per-
sistence of the beauty-sense. So much may with
modesty, in the light of present psychology, be
claimed for judgments upon literary art. And
this position should be taken sturdily against those
who would upset all canons and plead for the un-
licensed expression of personality. A technique of
the art—however it may have changed with the
change of ideal—has always and must always
exist.

But to go further and argue for changeless laws
entirely outside the human mind which makes and
accepts them, is dangerous.

Modern criticism, then, is aware of this general
change of front towards canons hitherto held to
be absolute and invariable; and its increased subjectivity, with the substitution of the personal impression for the historical laws, is more than individual whim, being in accord with a widespread
and typical intellectual process. It is not wise,

therefore, to regard this subjective tendency of criticism as egoistic in a bad sense. In its genesis, at bottom, such a habit is an instinct toward honesty. In the hands of the right sort of man the results of this manner of literary appreciation are both illuminating and stimulating. The reader catches the contagion of enthusiasm and receives a liberating sense of his own right to first-hand enjoyment. He makes bold to like a given piece of literature not because he must, but because it appeals to him, and here beginneth all truthful enjoyment in letters.

LITERATURE AS CRAFT

I

THE LOVE OF THE FINE PHRASE

The whole accomplishment, the whole desire of literature, may be resolved into the love for the fine phrase. Alfred de Musset once confessed, half-shamefacedly, his deep joy in phrasing; and always to the true maker in letters what is of supreme importance is the way one says things. To lavish infinite pains upon the manner of one's work is to be of the elect. We call Frenchmen like Flaubert and the De Goncourts men-of-letters, *par excellence,* just because this was with them a consuming ambition,—to seek the fittest, finest, most impeccable expression. More than is perhaps realized, the fine phrase makes the difference between platitude and the play of genius. Lowell has discoursed wisely of this, pointing out that what seems a striking thought becomes, on analysis, a striking medium for the conveyance of a thought which, less richly, less graciously, less boldly dressed, would be catalogued as a commonplace. Times innumerable, matter and manner are thus confused.

The usual sneer at this love for the fine phrase imputes shallowness and a worship of the æsthetic

divorced from the intellectual and the ethical.
The imputation is unfair and may, by a return
thrust, itself be called shallow. For the fine phrase
implies the fine personality behind it: an individuality of interest, a happy gift, a force not of
earth's predicable creatures. Literary style, while
it may be striven for and though it waits on wor-
shipful toil, cannot be commanded; its will is the
wind's will, after all. "When style revisits me,"
writes Robert Louis Stevenson, in those precious
"Vailima Letters," and he said it all in four
words. A craftsman he was, if ever one wielded
English speech; but he knew that diction would
come with inspiration, not before. With all his
cunning, he was not its master; style was his
mistress, to be wooed and won, an eternal feminine. In the physical world motion generates
heat and light; in the psychical world heat and
light are generated by emotion. And heat and
light are the wings of style.

It may seem to some a poor quest, this of the
fine phrase. The communication of ideas being
the most obvious mission of language, is there not
something puerile, even piddling, in an aspiration
for the right marshalling of words? Can this be
a valid life-work for grown men and women?
Verily, yes. For to make fine phrases is to create
beauty; and to create beauty is to have commerce
with the Eternal,—mortality's highest privilege.
Then, too, fine phrases inevitably are associated
with fine ideas—those apian miracles which at the

chance clangor of a word swarm in the brain-hive and deposit their amber sweets for the writer's behoof—and for posterity's.

Moreover, the power of the fine phrase is greater among men than they are aware, the fascination of style likely to be belittled. Even the Philistine, who would be first to pooh-pooh our glorification of diction, is moved, albeit unaware, by the apt turn, the smooth flow of the sentence, the sudden flash of metaphor, the musical cadence, the startling felicity of antithesis. He is subtly pleased, he reads on and on, and thinks, good easy man, it is little to do, that he is most concerned with mind-stuff. Ah, the agonies, the long trying, the failures innumerous, the despaired-of perfections that are back of and under that easy accomplishment. Mayhap our Philistine deems pleasure but a trifling thing to strive for, and hence puts the pleasuremaker on a par with the mountebank. Yet let him be honest with himself, and he shall find that pleasure—joy, happiness, the name matters not—is life's one conceivable guerdon, the only key to the mystery of mortality. To give pleasure to the knowing few is to be an artist, and the fine phrase is one of the legitimate artistic methods of pleasure-giving. Since all men, according to their light and degree of culture, are a-search for pleasure, and many find it in that fit and beautiful expression of personality which we call style in literature, the function of the fine phrase is justified; for it is seen to take its place in the economy of nature, meeting a real demand. To the serious artist in words, it is little less than a religion, this cult of the fine phrase. Here he will not sin, whatever he do in his daily walks. This temple he will not profane, the spirit that presides over it being august, lovely, without stain. Such a place is meet, he must fain feel, for his choicest sacrifices.

II

What is Literary Merit?

The things which in a deep sense we know and understand best are hardest to define. Love is the greatest motor-power on the earth, the common experience and the common glory of mankind. Yet who dares define it, to set a mete and a bound for humanity's master-passion? It is somewhat thus with such an intangible quality or characteristic as excellence in letters; we apprehend it readily enough, we mourn its absence, we thrill under a consciousness of its charm, but we are dazed a little at first when the question is put, plump and direct: What, then, is literary merit?

To come boldly at the difficulty, literary merit is that quality in writing which relates, not to the things said, but to the manner of saying things. It is, strictly speaking, a matter of form, and nothing else.

Emerson is literature, not because he is a great thinker in ethics or philosophy, but because he utters his thoughts in a certain beautiful and in-communicable fashion. The Bible, entirely apart from its value as a religious teacher, is a wonder-ful literary repository, simply because a set of men back in the early seventeenth century, when the diction of Marlowe and of Shakspere, of Ben Jonson and of Beaumont and Fletcher was in the air, were inspired to put its proverbs, its parables and its psalms into such language as has never been equaled in English before or since. If this defini-tion be correct, it becomes evident that books lying outside of what is called belles-lettres may have literary merit. When one who has a genius for expression writes, for example, upon science, he still makes literature; as witness a Humboldt or a Huxley. Whenever or wherever a man sets down his thoughts in a way which attracts, moves and charms by its style, or its manner of saying things, that man has literary merit, and no man else can be said to possess it.

Some may perhaps incline to take offense at this simple explanation of literary excellence. "What," they will cry, "the great effects of literature, the brilliancy and beauty, the wit and pathos, which have so often held us thrall, all this to be resolved into a trick of the trade, a legerdemain of rhe-toric?"

The answer to such an outbreak is not far to seek. Expression, at its best and in its normal function, is not a self-conscious act in which the writer stands off and strives to produce an impression, but is, rather, in some degree, a revelation; so that each man who makes literature gives the world, in his writings, a sort of simulacrum of his own personality, of that essence which is he, as against every other personality in existence. Nay, it is more than a simulacrum, for the whole creature is in it, brain and body, heart and soul. From his manner of saying things you gather an idea of what manner of man he is; not so much what he is in actual, every-day life as what he is potentially, in his possibilities, according as God made him.

But in setting up this definition of literary merit, it may still be objected that no true touchstone has been given to guide one in pronouncing for or against a man's claim to write literature. Granted that the manner of saying things is the test, how may this manner be distinguished? what are its earmarks? the elements or characteristics which go to make it? Perhaps the most common reply to this highly pertinent question is to catalogue, as do the rhetoricians, those qualities which are admirable in and essential to good writing: as simplicity, fitness and beauty, perspicuity, force and elegance, and so forth. But the trouble here is, that opinions are apt to differ as to what is beauty, or elegance, or force.

Perspicuity, clearness, common folk might agree pretty well on; but when we come to the other qualities, there is sure to be confusion worse confounded. When a stump orator out West told a friend of mine that he had read Bunyan's "Pilgrim's Progress" and found it interesting, but that it had no literary merit, he showed that his sense of the qualities that go to the making of such merit was erratic, half-developed.

A housemaid the other day informed me that a missing article was in "the nurse's apartment." Now, the place she referred to was a small, plainly furnished room of perhaps ten by twelve feet. To call it "an apartment" was absurd, because that word gave a false idea of its fitting-up and of its size. The word "room" would have been better, because fitter and simpler; moreover, because it is a native Saxon word and hence preferable to the Romance word, "apartment," which is used unnecessarily and wrongly in nine cases out of ten.

These examples serve to illustrate my point, which is, that it is insufficient and dangerous to insist on a certain number of qualities as constituting the literary manner of saying things. Such categories are of avail in giving students a notion of what is to be aimed at in writing; but they are not satisfactory in defining what is style —that subtle and wonderful thing. That an observance of the laws of grammar is at the basis of style hardly needs the saying; such observance leads to correct writing, but not necessarily to the producing of literature, any more than the foundation walls of a building settle the question of its subsequent architectural ugliness or beauty. I would choose a more subjective test than that of

the rhetorics, and would affirm that a perception
of the manner of saying things which constitutes
literary merit can only be reached by a constant
and catholic reading of the best literature.

By heredity one can have almost an intuition
of what is good, so that the life's reading is begun
with a great advantage over another who has no
bookish ancestry; but even the latter can acquire
this sixth sense by dint of wise and multifarious
contact with books. The stump orator could not
see the beauty of Bunyan simply for the reason
that he had not got into his blood the rhythm of
fine prose, nor a feeling for the virile strength of
Saxon methods of expression. My maid thought
"apartment" more high-sounding and aristocratic
than "room," because she had not read enough
and heard enough good speech to learn the great
lesson that in both written and spoken words,
other things being equal, the simplest is always
the best.

By constant and intelligent communion with
the master spirits of English letters, and then, if
possible, with those of foreign literature, the reader
comes to recognize intuitively and with perfect
ease the distinction and charm of manner which
make literature. He learns, too, that the manner
itself may vary almost as often as do the men
who speak; that Addison and Carlyle both write
literature, yet are at the antipodes of style; that
the glory of Walt Whitman is one and the glory
of Tennyson is another. Yet will he discover that

all have somewhat in common, though with infinite variations and manifold divergencies; that all possess a common gift and a common distinction which lead us to declare them makers of literature and masters of the mighty art of letters.

Coming back, then, to our starting point, literary merit lies in the manner of saying things. Original thought, noble conception, poetic imagining, these are precious; but unless they be poured into the transmuting mold of expression they are not of themselves enough to constitute literature. And the way to gain the power of knowing this great gift of expression is for the reader to acquaint himself or herself with the books pronounced by the calm, sure judgment of the centuries to be the best and most worthy to live— books that possess what Austin Dobson has called "Time's great antiseptic, style." And in the case of the writer, this same reading should be supplemented by a steady, unwearying use of the pen, since only thus will it gradually acquire a power mightier than the sword, even as persuasion is mightier than violence and the shaping of souls more than the mutilation of the body.

III

MUSIC AND EMOTION IN POETRY

Alliteration, or the rhyming of initial letters, is a device which, used either in prose or poetry, is likely to be despised and misunderstood by those who incline to snap-judgments. This is due in part to ignorance, in part to the patent abuse of alliteration, as seen, for example, in the head-lines of sensational journalism, or, if literature be in evidence, in the verse of such a man as Swin-burne, whose alliterative *tours de force* are alone in modern poetry for self-consciousness and per-sistency. But the fact is—and it is well to em-phasize and illustrate it—that alliteration is a thing of historical dignity in English verse (and English prose as well), and is, moreover, in es-sence and primarily a psychic phenomenon.

Let me show what is meant, first, as to the his-tory of this characteristic of the technique of po-etry, confining the discussion to verse, as the form of literature wherein alliteration is most plainly to be seen in its workings. As is well known to students of English verse, alliteration precedes rhyme in the historical development of our native poetry. Rhyme (which is the sound-agreement of words at the end of a line in contradistinction from the initial-letter rhyming which we call allit-eration) came into English from the medieval Latin hymns through the French, and we do not find it used till long after the Norman Conquest. But for centuries before this, poetry was culti-vated as an art, and had its definite, artistic laws and formularies; and the particular device which was the predecessor of rhyme as a means of music-making (which is, as we shall see in a moment, the object both of rhyme and alliteration) is alliteration. Let me illustrate from a famous Anglo-Saxon poem, the epic of "Beowulf," our first great English epic. The following is a typical line from the poem:

> "Oft Scyld Scefing Sceathena threatum"—
> Often Scyld, son of Scef, with troops of warriors—.

Here, be it observed, we find three alliterative words, and, noting the literal translation placed under the line, we see that those words are important noun-words. Now, without going into the minutiæ of the matter, it is sufficient to say that the normal Anglo-Saxon line of poetry is built in this way, showing two alliterations in the first half of the verse and one at least in the second half, and that the accents fall on the alliterative word, which is necessarily an important one in both grammar and meaning. There are subdivisions and finesses of this main law, such as to make the construction of old English verse a highly wrought and intricate affair. And yet here is a poem whence the illustration is drawn, written presumably in the seventh or eighth century, hundreds of years before rhyme, as now understood, was dreamed of in English. How foolish and ignorant, in the face of such data, to speak of the earliest English poetry, and of art in this field, as rough and inartistic! Nevertheless so it is treated in the majority of manuals on English literature.

In a word, then, alliteration, instead of being a more or less flimsy trick of the trade in poetry, is an art-law which reigned supreme for centuries in our older and noble poetic products, and which, moreover, I want to show is still a legitimate and even necessary device and aid to expression when rightly used. All the best modern verse proves this, and I shall try to make this plain under my second thesis, namely, that alliteration is a psychic phenomenon, and hence is an inevitable accompaniment to true and inspired poetry.

For consider for a moment that both rhyme and alliteration, as hinted above, are means of securing music in the poem; this is their sole *raison d'être*. Rhyme, by the consonance of vowels and consonants, and by more definitely marking the rhythm of the verse, adds to the musicalness thereof; and alliteration, by the repetition of identical letters rhythmically distributed in a line, produces likewise an effect of music and a desirable tone-color, less full and rich, however, than rhyme, but nevertheless a musical effect. Now the next thing to notice is the interesting and perfectly demonstrable dictum that in poetry there is a direct relation between emotion and music; that is, a poet makes music in so far as he is emotionally vibrant and alive. But if alliteration be one way of gaining an effect of music, it follows logically that the singer emotionally creative will instinctively and of necessity make use of alliteration as one means of securing the desired result.

This explains what I mean in stating that alliteration is a psychic phenomenon; it is an outward and visible token of an inward (subjective) and poetic state or condition on the part of the bard. If we accept this definition—and it seems to be a sound and philosophical one—we are in a position at once to understand the true function of this so often disesteemed characteristic of formal poetry, and, with this touchstone, to pronounce on what is good or bad in alliteration. Alliteration is, then, a mark of emotion, and its effect is to add music to the poet's work. If a spurt of lyric feeling tends to alliterative language this should be apparent in both prose and poetry. As a matter of fact it is apparent; and, confining myself still to verse, I will give an example or two.

Once on a time Walter Savage Landor wrote a splendid piece of blank verse to Robert Browning, beginning:

> "Shakespeare is not our poet, but the world's,
> Therefore of him, no speech."

And the praise herein tendered by the golden-tongued classicist to the chief dramatic singer of our century, culminates with a marked sibilant alliteration in the lines:

> "Beyond Sorrento and Amalfi, where
> The siren waits thee, singing song for song."

The artistic climax calls for and produces an alliterative richness lacking, and rightly lacking, in the preceding lines. Hence, this is an example of what may be called legitimate, organic alliteration; by which is meant, alliteration corresponding with the march and culmination of the poem. In the superb little lyric, "Home Thoughts from Abroad," the bard here apostrophized by Landor furnishes another example:

> "And after April, when May follows,
> And the whitethroat builds, and all the swallows!
> Hark, where my blossomed pear-tree in the hedge
> Leans to the field and scatters on the clover
> Blossoms and dewdrops—at the bent spray's edge—
> That's the wise thrush; he sings each song twice over,
> Lest you should think he never could recapture
> The first fine careless rapture!"

And in those two closing lines notice the double alliteration on *f* and *c,* so distributed as to produce the finest effect. The climax, which is more emotional than in Landor's blank verse, is an impulsive leap of creative expression and lo! alliteration comes to enrich the language use and deepen the music. It is not "alliteration's artful aid" here, but something far more natural and significant. Indeed, that line, "alliteration's artful aid," has done harm no end in spreading this misconception that alliteration is always a self-conscious and technical affair, never psychic, personal and spontaneous. It is worth noting that the four additional lines in this poem of Browning's have almost an effect of anticlimax, after the splendid alliterative and emotional crest of feeling in the passage just quoted.

Examples might be multiplied indefinitely, for all literature is full of them. The principle which is evolved from such modern instances seems to be that the right kind of alliteration comes in spurts correspondent to emotive impulses, and will be, consequently, irregular and not regular in occurrence. This is the reason why the alliteration of Swinburne strikes a false note so often and becomes offensive at times. That great poet makes use of the device almost as systematically as did the Anglo-Saxon gleemen, with whom, as was shown, it was a definite, artistic law of poetics. In other words, alliteration with Swinburne is not inevitably conjoined with lyric intensity, but is used coldly, self-consciously. Hence, a sense in the reader that it is artificial. It ceases to have dynamic, psychic significancy, and becomes a purely formal and sensuous enrichment or ornamentation of the verse. Let me give a single illustration. In "Anactoria," a certain passage ends with the line,

"Memories shall mix and metaphors of me."

Here it hardly needs saying that both thought and phraseology preclude the possibility of an emotional state; yet the *m* alliteration is excessive. Thousands of examples of this tendency in the author of "Laus Veneris" could be cited. I do not for a moment mean to say that plenty of Swinburne's poems might not be mentioned in which a masterful handling of alliteration is linked with

the most fervent feeling and an irresistibly song-
ful lilt. But, speaking by and large, an effect of
artificiality is indubitably made by Swinburne's
technique in this particular, and he offers the most
striking modern instance of the abuse of one of
the oldest art laws in English poetry, and deserves
careful study with this single characteristic in
mind.

"Yes," objects the critic, "but why is it worse
for Swinburne to use alliteration thus consciously
and steadily than for the Anglo-Saxons to do so,
as you have confessed they did?" The answer is
that to the Old English bard this method of music-
making was what rhyme is now in English verse;
but Swinburne, in addition to a lavish and wonderful use of rhyme music, superadds this music
of alliteration, and the result is a cloying richness, an over-lusciousness which is often dwelt
upon in any analysis of his work.

A man who has Swinburne's intense love of his
art and a supreme gift for music in verse, and
whose handling of alliteration is marked yet
sharply divergent from the English poet's inas-
much as it is natural and correspondent to emotion, not artificial and formal, is Sidney Lanier.
The flush and fire of much of his lyric work is
brought about, among other things, by his alliterative prodigality. But a study of him will reveal
the distinction made between him and a Swinburne in this regard. Take his perfect song "The
Dove" and let us look at the closing stanza:

"Nay, if ye three, O Morn! O Spring! O Heart!
Should chant grave unisons of grief and love,
Ye could not mourn with more melodious art
Than daily doth yon dim sequestered dove."

Here there is a strong alliterative effect, secured by the *m* and *d* rhymes of the two verses that bring the lyric to a close. Here, also, is a distinct rhetorical and lyrical climax of a subtly quiet but strong and lovely sort. This may be realized by any one who reads the three preceding stanzas which lead up to the comparison whose quintessence is expressed in these closing lines. Therefore, this is a classic example of fit and spontaneous alliteration. The one law of right use is, as Lanier himself has said, that the poet be honest; by which he meant that he be not self-conscious, nor his linguistics and metrics studied at the moment of composition. Sidney Lanier is alliterative to an extent without parallel among American poets (unless Poe be excepted), but only because his genius was intensely lyrical and he was a natural music-maker. Swinburne, contrariwise, while also a true and exquisite lyrist, has made the mistake of riding alliteration to death, forcing it to become a set, formal law in his work; and so we hear, too often, the creak of the machinery coming in to disturb the God-given melody of his song.

Our study of alliteration then, even thus in brief, leads to a very decided opinion and to firm ground of theory. It is, we see, a thing of legitimacy and of great importance in the development of English poetry—indeed, of all poetry. It is not a pretty verbal trick to tickle our ears withal, but, rather, is inwrought with the being of man when he is creatively inspired to literary pro- duction. It is, to be sure, capable of abuse, as is well exemplified in the case of Swinburne; but, in its purity and right use, it constitutes one of the chief beauties of the technique of poetry. Ex- actly the same line of argument can be applied to prose, and illustrations are legion from our best prose writers. It can also be shown that allitera- tion in maxims and proverbs has both a mnemonic and an artistic function. But this is a subject by itself. In our mighty prose authors it will be found that their places and periods of rhetorical climax and creative splendor are rich with alliter- ation at its finest and freest.

However, the discussion has here been limited to verse, and I repeat as a summary: Alliteration in any serious study of English poetry must be re- garded as a mark of emotion, a psychic phenom- enon, having definite and close relations to the spirit of the man who seizes on it instinctively as an aid to and ornament of expression.

INDOORS AND OUT: TWO REVERIES

I

BEFORE THE FIRE

What a walk is in the early spring woods, with its chance of finding the trailing arbutus shy-hid beneath the dead brown leaves or of thrilling again at the sight of the stainless white bloom of the bloodroot, such to midwinter is the indoor open fire on the hearth. Twin delights these, each after its kind, growing with the years and fuller associations.

To-day, returning from the city, I note the bleakness of the western sky and hear in the intermittent wind-gust a doleful presage of storm and a shut-in frozen world on the morrow. But my thoughts outfly me homeward, and I pluck up heart at the image that is evoked of a cheery blaze and a backlog that gravely drones a soothing bass to the vibrant, nervous treble of the flames aspiring, striving, and at last paling down to embers and eventual ashes. And even so the reality. That mundane matter, dinner, dispatched, and slippers donned, I am in front of the polished andirons that twinkle reflections of the facile lights. Cozy in my big Sleepy-Hollow armchair, I can listen in a very unction of creature comfort

to the somber wail or leonine roar of the wind outside, enjoying vicariously for all less lucky
mortals.

What a long, weary journey has civilized man
taken since the first fire of like kind was lighted
for enheartenment against darkness, cold, hunger,
loneliness! And yet, with the vast deal that has
been learned and sloughed off and forgotten, back
he comes to this primitive solace to find it all-
sufficing and, in truth, the acme of nineteenth-
century luxury. The thought has its reproof, its
warning. But since the day our forefathers piled
high the great rough-hewn branches in the hall
and quaffed ale and mead from curiously chased
cups as the flames licked lithely toward the smoke
dark rafters, much has entered imaginatively into the wood fire as a fact in life, to broaden and
enrich its content and suggestion. The literature
of our own country has thrown on many a stick
to yield a more ethereal glow. The wood fire has
put on a mystic aspect since Poe wrote his "Raven"
before it:

> And each separate dying ember
> Wrought its ghost upon the floor.

Longfellow's "Tales of a Wayside Inn" had never
crept so warmly into our affections had it not
been the emanation of the group about the backlog. Hawthorne, too, in his wonder-tales, needs
to be read with this sibilant, colorful background.
And what were the gentle imaginings of Ik Mar-

vel, without a fire to look deep into and to search
for his source of inspiration. Nor can we unseat
Mr. Warner from his ingle quarters, emitting wit
and wisdom as the wood emits sparks and suffus-
ing the atmosphere with the steadfast radiance
of a kindly heart, even as the clear blue flame from
the driftwood lights up the room, making it homely and habitable. These and other like mages of
the pen have, with a potent species of wizardry,
made every flame-spurtle emblematic and each
stage in this conflict of the elements *in petto* a
precious thing to see and to remember.

When the fire is high and the crackle of the
hickory as merry a sound as the gleam thereof is
cheery, playing hide-and-seek in the uttermost
corners of the study, a sense of housed satisfaction, of sensual warmth and lazy peace, unite to
make a mood of serene though inexpressive pleasure. But as the logs give up inchwise their sturdy
length, and are resolved into a charred and broken
semblance of their sometime selves, the mood
shifts into reminiscence, reverie, and so shades
imperceptibly into melancholy. This pensive
state, this rôle of "Il Penseroso," is a sort of
natural outflow of the precedent stage of quiescent
delight. Wordsworth speaks of:

> That sweet mood when pleasant thoughts
> Bring sad thoughts to the mind;

and this well describes what goes on in my soul
before the fire. Now, see, my eyes are fathoms

deep in the glowing coals, ruby red and scintillating like the irises of a snake, while for a setting all around is the soft, harmonious, dreamy gray of the ashes. How at peace they are and how beautiful, after the brief fury and festal display of the fire! Is it true, then, that this is the inevitable issue of motion and color, warmth and fragrant odor and pleasances of song? In pursuance of the somber thought I reach out to the bookcase, take down Schopenhauer from the shelf, and read a passage wherein the Apostle of Negation eloquently apostrophizes that giving up of life and the lust of life which alone, he deems, offers a solution of the stress and agony of human things. If he be right, the quintessence of wisdom has been exemplified in the burning of these branches from the forest which grows outside my window.

They have had their moment of keen, vivid life, but, lest activity become torture and zest satiety, they have exchanged restlessness for sleep and annihilation. Purged in the fierce purgation of flame, theirs is the stainless lot and the Nirvana which is good. By irresistible analogy the mind takes up the mortal case and the age-old query, What of Life beyond? knocks at the door of consciousness with dreary insistence. More often than not when such questions come we blink at them, turning away with some ready excuse or so immersed in the hour's duties that such-like problems are put aside for the nonce, to be taken up

at some pat opportunity. We are fully aware that
the riddle for us is still unsolved; we believe honestly that some day it will be proved in grim earnest. But alas! the continual putting off acts like
a narcotic, until indifference is begotten and we
drift along with no clear notion where the path
ends or whither it would lead us. We have put
the question so carefully away for future reference, that it is lost; even as o'er-careful house-
wives, for safe keeping, hide something delectable
or necessary, belonging to the male side of the
house—hide it so successfully that it is not forth-
coming in the hour of necessity.   *   *   *

The last red eye has winked itself into oblivion
now and, Schopenhauer closed but still on my
lap, I still sit and muse above the once ardent
ashes. Musing thus, listening to the wind moan-
ing about the house gables, is it not the forecast
of old age, when the tension shall relax and the
vision dim, while slowly the cold of stagnant blood
creeps upward until the vital parts are reached
and all is over? The air of the room chills, and
my heart stirs with a vague loneliness, as of the
forsaken. But such gray fancies, true mates of
the ashes, are not my normal way of meditation,
and finally I spring up as the clock below stairs
strikes twelve with musical iteration. I build me
in a trice another fire and marking what a goodly
bed the former blaze has left for its successor,
I say in dumb argument with my critical ego:
"This has been no annihilation; here is substitu-

tion, not destruction; nothing is lost in this translation of the wood; the phenomenal aspect of the
process is a mere eye-cheat and, dealt with by
either reason or faith, there is no cause for me-
grims or mooning." And, comforted at heart, I
brood on until the first faint twitter of birds her-
alds the coming of the hopeful dawn that shall
bring a new day of work and growth and worship.

II

When the Sap Runs Up in the Trees

It seems somewhiles, at the turn of the year, as
if the time of buds and birds would never come.
New England is famous for this hesitant mood,
this chariness in surrendering her wintry fortress
to the winsome season for which man waits and
yearns.

Late in March I stand and look across the fields
that lie as barren and bleak as ever they did in
mid December. The left-over leaves of yesteryear
hang in straggling bunches and splashes on beech
boughs and elms, ghostly pale; you would say they
never could be shaken off by the wind, or pushed
aside when the vital sprouts of the new year
prick their way into sight. It is a time for faith,
hope, and charity. The air is raw and harsh;
the clouds lower gloomily, and as like as not a
nor'easter settles down for several days on end,
the fittest thing possible in this monochrome of

cold grays and unlustrous browns. After the storm, I stroll along the river bank; the face of nature still betokens a sombre mood, and the fields are as before, dreary-colored, the trees gaunt skeletons creaking like gallows that dangle corpses in their air graves on high. But of a sudden, my eye catches the hue of the alders that grow beside the stream, and my heart gives a great thump of joy; for lo! the branches are a flare of dull, strange, dusky yellow, a note of spring, so indefinite, so out of sympathy with the landscape round about, as to make almost an impression of the uncanny, the supernatural. And, next day, walking down the stately avenue, I am aware that the arching boughs of the soft maples have thrown a branched redness on the air, signet of the sprouting tide, and so welcome with their mass of rich bold color that one is tempted to idleness beneath their pleached pleasance. And these signs, mark you, are before the general carnival of sounds and sights, when every fool knows it is spring, and a song on the lips is the meet way of praise. As yet, bleakness, gray tints, and inhospitable suns.

But a week later comes a change; a really bland day, mild and soft with south winds, and filtered through and thorough-through with sunshine,— a miracle to answer the doubt and fear bred of Nature's sphinx-like manner of silence as to her intentions. It is too good to be verity, and I pinch myself to make sure I am all awake. The-

oretically, I knew spring would arrive, and that
once come she would be companioned by beauty.
But oh, treacherous memory, knowing is one
thing, and feeling a magical other! I had forgotten how sweet was the smell of the succulent
new grass, how silver-blithe the robin at my
morning window, how ineffably tender the green
of the leafing trees. The shades, transitions,
chromatic nuances of this spring foliage; who
has ever expressed their charm and loveliness?
They are as ethereal as colors seen in dreams, yet
as fresh and splendidly vivid as the first flower
of Eden's garden. Gaze at the willow, for example, until that delicate ravishment of budding
life is part of you, and then let your vision feed
on the dark emerald of the lawn uplit by yellow
splashes of sun; what a contrast, what exhaustless pleasure of shifting tints and tones, and all
within the gamut of a single color, nature's summer favorite! And peach and cherry trees, too,
are aburst with blossoms, pink, perfect, scattering
odors as a wind-puff scatters leaves; the apple
boughs will follow soon and add their virginal
whiteness to the orchard symphony. Then how
the birds respond to the lure of the sun! It will
be high tide with them before one is awake, for
even to-day, listening, you shall hear bobolinks,
grosbeaks, and orioles, in full chorus. A robin, fat
and familiar in his gayety of livery, alights on
the ground only a few feet off, and with head
a-cock lets one admire his splendor of waistcoat

and the smug proportions of one who is the pride
of his family. And in early evening, the thrush-
note floats down from among the tree-tops like a
voice from the other side of the year. The first
twilights out-of-doors, how good they are, what
mystic hours of revery and sweet illusion! Once
again the frogs are at it in the pond, and the vast,
vocal night takes their croaking and blends it in
with the other nocturnal noises, by some wonder-
work making a many-voiced music.

When the moon rolls up from the nether east
to make fairyland of the wood, and shows us our
dear ones sitting by our side draped in soft cling-
ing white stuffs and with uncovered hair, upon
which the dews fall harmless, and from which
exhale the rich scents of some exotic of the south,
how sense-enthralling yet spiritual is the hour!
Hark, that you may pick out, in the orchestra of
night, the pellucid obligato of the little stream
yonder in the bottom glade. For now are the
waters loosened, every brook overflows, and from
sources innumerable, swollen by snows wherever
pines make shade, and hoar and cavernous rocks
elude the sun's touch, the rivulets turn torrents,
and what was yesterday a barren place to-day
promises fair pasturage for flocks and herds. That
sweet-sounding phrase, "the sound of many
waters," came to the singer on some such time
and tide as this, when spring wrought marvels
with the land, and Nature donned her festal robes
after the sack-cloth and ashes of hibernation. If

one be a veritable worshipper of Pan, may not
the murmur of the sap running up in the trees be
heard distinctlier the more of love is in the soul?
A gentle, mellow sound it is, an overtone of joy
to the graver doings of earth and sky. Some day
now I shall uncover deep in the boscage the shy
pink blooms and the spicy fragrance of the arbutus, firstling of April flowers. Ah, Spring, of a
truth, thou art the Age of Gold come again;
eternal youth is in thy buoyant paths, and mortal
man must be enamoured of thee until the end of
ends.